C++

C++ BASICS FOR BEGINNERS

Andy Vickler

Table of Contents

Introduction

C++ is a computer language that may be put to a multitude of uses—developed as an extension of the C programming language to include an object-oriented paradigm, which is derived from the C programming language. It's a compiled and imperative language at the same time, which is nice. It's an intermediate language with the advantage of being able to develop low-level drivers as well as kernels, desktop apps, games, GUI, etc. At the same time, programmers are of a higher level. The grammar and structure of code in the languages C and C ++ are fundamentally the same.

C ++ is indeed a versatile programming language accompanied by a wide range of capabilities. It may be used to create operating systems, browsers, games, and a variety of other applications. Procedural, object-oriented, and functional programming is just a few of the programming paradigms supported by C ++. Because of this, C ++ is both strong and adaptable. The most essential thing to remember while studying C ++ is to keep your attention on the topics. The purpose of learning programming is to improve your programming skills, which means being more successful at implementing and designing the latest systems and keeping existing systems in the long run. C ++ is capable of supporting a wide range of programming techniques. You may write in any language in the manner of FORTRAN, C, Smalltalk, and other programming languages.

Each style is capable of accomplishing its objectives while retaining runtime and space effectiveness. Hundreds of millions of developers use C ++, and it's used in practically every application segment. C ++ is widely utilized in the development of drivers of devices and other software that depends on direct hardware manipulation while operating in strict period limitations. Because it is clean enough to allow for effective teaching of fundamental ideas, the frequent use of C ++ is for training and researching. Almost everyone who has worked with a Macintosh computer or a Windows-based computer has come into contact with C ++ on some level since the principal UI of both systems is in C ++.

Chapter 1

Everything You Need to Know About Computer Programming

To get the most of your programming language learning experience, it will be beneficial for you to first grasp what programming is and how it works, as well as some of the programming vocabulary involved. A computer on its own is a pointless piece of equipment. It's nothing more than a collection of several hardware components integrated into a single device. At this point, none of the hardware parts, whether they are used collectively or separately, are useful. This is comparable to the quality of a car that has been constructed. Is the automobile of any use if the gasoline tank is empty? Similar to this, we must feed the computer with fuel, in this instance, electrical power to function properly (Although there were some new mechanical systems, we're talking about electrical devices here.)

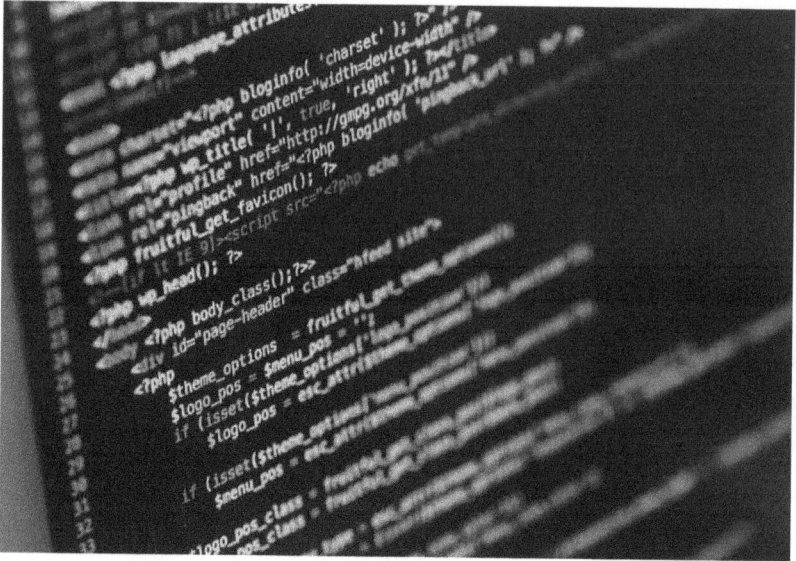

At this stage, a system is effectively nothing more than a jumble of small electrical switches that can only be turned on or off. This is like with adequate gasoline and the ability to drive, however, there are no drivers available to drive. We need a driver who is capable of using the steering wheel, gears, brakes, and other controls that allow the vehicle to move. Similar to this, by configuring various switches in various configurations, we may direct these computers for doing a certain action, such as playing a movie on the screen or playing music via the computer speakers, or opening a file, among other things. It is, in other words, nothing more than directing a computer on how to operate these switches, when to operate them, and when they should operate. In a nutshell, this is what programming is, in its most basic form.

The term "programming" is often used to refer to computer programming. And with that, we arrive at our first and most essential question! Creating and creating computer programs is the procedure of developing and designing computer programs. Isn't it a rather obvious explanation? At its most fundamental level, programming can be thought of as the process of delivering instructions to a computer to do a task you need - This may appear to be quite similar to which way you use your computer. Simply said, the distinction between what you are performing today as a computer user and what you'll be doing in the future and the instructions are kept somewhere and may be reused as required, which is what you might be performing as a programmer. You have engaged in some form of computer programming if you've ever worked with macros in a software application, including a processor word and spreadsheet (or any of the myriad other programs that are macro capable). It is simple like as a set of instructions that are stored in a text file to perform certain common tasks, such as backing up a folder containing all computer files, or something more complicated like a word processor or application used by your computer, it may require millions of lines of code, programs coming in all shapes and sizes. We must realize that computers, which are normally made up of silicon, plastic, metal, and other sticky materials, that allow them to do amazing things that seem imaginative, cannot imagine themselves. Instead, they can process information. They do not, however, understand how to follow instructions. So, what exactly are these commands? It comes to the level of detail that a computer can comprehend. These must be extremely precise, detailed, and complete instructions. They should be in a form that the computer's processor and other components can interpret- which are little electrical pulses that humans are unable to produce (at least not at this time). In some respects, a computer program may be compared to a recipe, a series of instructions that may be followed to achieve a certain outcome. If you're following a recipe, keep in mind that the directions were written by a human and maybe a touch wordy, leaving out certain details. The person is supposed to know what a blender is, where it can be found, how to set it up, and how to use it. It is also assumed that the human understands what the terms pour and frothy imply and how to use them correctly, etc. It is envisaged that the human chef would fill in the gaps. This is impossible for a computer to do since, other than a few very basic commands, it has no understanding of what is being spoken. This is accomplished by providing a means for humans to write instructions that can subsequently be translated into something that computers can comprehend (or vice versa). In computing, a programming language is defined as a "method of instructions writing." It is possible to create computer instructions in a human-readable programming language and then have those instructions converted into a language that a machine can comprehend.

The commands that people understand are often referred to as (you guessed it) code! In the computer world, each line of human-readable code turns out to be hundreds of complex instructions. This translation is accomplished through the use of specific software (or a combination of programs) - There are translators for each computer language, who are referred to as editors or interpreters. When the translation is completed, the output is saved in a certain format, such as a file or group of files (or in-memory storage in some situations), and instructions will be followed by the computer and (hopefully) perform the desired function each time the software is run. Despite the common misconception that you must be a genius to build effective software, almost anyone who knows a computer and is interested can learn to edit if you want to become a power user. Ordinary people with special knowledge and skills write most computer software. While mastering computer programming can be a lifelong endeavor, gaining the necessary knowledge and skills to be able to perform useful tasks is not impossible for everyone who understands how to operate a computer and is prepared to put in a little time or a lot of effort, but is still unable to achieve

1.1 What is Computer Programming

Programming is often identified as coding. It is the skill of instructing a system to complete a task that you have set out for it to perform. Programming, in its most basic definition, is the act of writing programs. It's simply a set of commands designed to inform the computer systems to perform each specific task. Depending on its application, a program is also known as a computer program or a software application. Because a computer is only hardware, it needs instructions to function. These instructions are carried out by the computer's central processing unit (CPU). The process of identifying how to solve an issue is known as programming. No matter what technique is used to solve a problem — a pencil and paper, a slide rule, an adding machine, or a computer are all options for solving requires preparation. According to the definition above, programming is the process of determining how to solve a problem.

The computer will solve the issue for us in this case. Thus we are not truly solving the problem. If we solve the issue ourselves, we will not be required to build a program, and as a result, we will not need a system. Is that not right? So, why do we require a computer? It's only that we distinguish how to fix an issue and also how to tell a machine to do it for us, but we are unable to do it at the speed and precision that a computer is capable of doing for us. We also get weary and sick with implementing the similar over and again, but the system could perform the same task zillions of times with the same speed and precision as the first time without being bored or exhausted. We may use the easy example of computing the Sum of all even integers from 1 to 1,000,000 to illustrate our point. Even while this is not impossible, the time necessary to calculate it as well as the chance of committing a blunder at some time, the number of resources required, whether we use a pen and paper or a calculator, as well as other similar considerations, make it an unattractive alternative. What if, in addition to this, we need to compute between distinct sets of integers regularly? Humanly speaking, it is challenging. We can, however, do this in less than 5 minutes by building a program to do it. Meanwhile, we can run the same program again and over again to do any number of computations, and we can receive correct answers in seconds by running the same program repeatedly. For example, I may command that each number be added to the next by a computer. And then add every following number to the previous total until we reach the upper limit that has been defined.

Don't worry about the precision of instructions; what you need to realize is that I can only teach a computer to assist in the solution of an issue if I understand how to do it myself. This indicates that unless I am aware of the answer to the issue, it is pointless for me to even attempt to solve one. Let us consider the case of an on-the-street cab driver who is a newcomer to town and needs directions. We can't just get in the vehicle and tell him to take us to Point A as we used to with the previous taxi driver. To ensure that he gets to his destination safely, we will have to provide him with detailed directions on how to get there. I can only provide him with travel directions if I am familiar with them. Unless this is done, it will be a fruitless endeavor. In the same manner, there is no use in even attempting to develop a program before you have a clear understanding of how you want to approach the issue in the first place. To put it another way, programming is the act of instructing a computer on what to perform. Even though it seems to be simple, it is quite sophisticated.

There are two things that you will need to keep in mind in this situation: The most crucial thing to remember about computers is that they do not communicate in English. Because a computer is a machine, it knows just two fundamental concepts: on and off. This is because computers are machines. The idea of on and off is referred to as an on represents one, and off represents zero in a binary system. Hence the computer understands just one language, the Binary language, which is composed of 0 and 1. The second most crucial thing to remember is that your directions must be EXACT. As previously stated, a computer on its own is a completely ineffective piece of equipment. It's nothing more than a collection of several hardware components integrated into a single device.

1.2 Advantages of a Career in Computer Programming

I'd want to share some of the advantages with you pursuing a career in computer programming, but first, let's take a brief look at what computer programming is and how it differs from other careers. The term "computer programming" can be defined in a variety of ways, but to make things as basic and as useful to our lives as necessary, I'd describe computer programming as the ability to create computer code to interact with computers in a language that they recognize so that they can complete certain jobs for humans. Operating a spreadsheet program, a word processor, and other comparable tasks are examples of these tasks that should be completed before using an email program on a daily basis. For example, before we can use a spreadsheet application, it must first be loaded and enabled by the computer that is hosting it. As soon as the application has been loaded and enabled, the computer is referred to as "running" it. As a result, the duty job of a computer programmer is to write the instructions that make up a spreadsheet program in a language understood by the computer. In the majority of cases, this vast collection of specific instructions is considered to be with a software program or a program. A significant increase in the number of possible consumers who want different applications has resulted from the fact that computers are far smaller and less expensive. They are also much more numerous to count than they were several decades earlier. What's more, because of the broad availability of the internet, a large number of these computers are now linked to one another.

As a result, considering a career in computer programming is something you should consider. However, it's not suited for everyone. But, if you do meet the requirements, you will be able to explore a whole new universe, with the only limitations being those imposed by your own creative and imaginative abilities. Listed below are a few of the advantages of choosing computer programming as a professional path: Computer programmers are in great demand, which increases their chances of landing a job or staying in a position if they currently have one in the industry. When working in this field, you will most likely discover that you have the opportunity of having flexible working hours. In many circumstances, there is the possibility of being able to work practically anywhere rather than being required to travel. We can never entirely avoid politics since we are human, and the programming area is typically a result-driven setting relatively than a political one. It has the potential to be a very rewarding professional path. There will be various opportunities to work on a range of projects with other like-minded people. If you're retired or want to be, you'll have the freedom to work on your own for long periods of time and to travel between different industries depending on your preferences and where you want to live. We have just scraped the surface of the subject here since there are other advantages to consider. It's possible to cover some of these topics in more depth, so keep an eye out. You can learn about computer programming, one of the most fascinating disciplines on the planet, if you approach it properly. Programming, in contrast to other key courses in school, should get a separate treatment. Beginning programmers must have a thorough grasp of how programming is done and what the fundamentals of the subject matter are before they can begin. Programming is essentially the act of instructing a computer to do a job. It's a lot like teaching a child how to add numbers for the first time.

When programming persons, we often use a variety of languages that the subject can comprehend, such as English or French. In the same manner, producing a computer program necessitates the use of computer-readable programming languages like Java, C, Pascal, and Python. These are written by humans. Human languages are very complicated, yet because of our intellect, we can learn how to communicate in them. Computers, on the other hand, are not very intelligent; the language used to educate them is quite basic. This is the reason why learning one or more computer programming languages may be both enjoyable and simple for a human being like you. Once you have been comfortable with one computer language, it will be much simpler for you to learn another shortly. Logic is often regarded as the foundation of every program. It must be constructed by the resources made available by your programming language of choice. Preparing the logic must be completed before the actual coding process can begin. Before you begin the process of building the software, you should create a flow plan for it or write the algorithm that will govern it. The vast majority of applications allow you to divide the software into different roles. These functions must be written in the shortest amount of time possible with the fewest number of instructions. Ideally, they should be constructed in such a manner that they may be repurposed regularly. The incorrect use of syntax is one of the most common causes of programming mistakes.

The syntax of each command, as well as the integral functions that you want to employ, may be checked using a variety of applications that offer the necessary functionality. The lower the number of instructions in a program, the quicker the pace it may be executed. When it comes to getting a job completed, we often use sophisticated reasoning. The fact that this work may be completed quickly and efficiently by using the built-in features of the programming language is something we were unaware of. You must be familiar with all of the built-in capabilities offered in the application to prevent these issues in the future. The usage of proper names in functions and variables makes the coding process much easier to complete. The use of illogical variable names will not impair the functioning of the program, but it will make it more difficult for you to improve or amend the code after it has been written. Aside from being familiar with different programming languages, computer programming for beginners entails becoming acquainted with the recommendations listed above. If you wish to pursue a profession in programming, you should keep these considerations in mind at all times. According to the majority of employment forecasters, computer programming training is one of the most promising educational paths in terms of future job prospects. A computer programming education, whether obtained via a standard college degree program or a certification course, may open numerous avenues for those looking for work seeking to get work in this continuously evolving profession. In the science of programming, which is exactly what it is, developers and inputters work together to create and input a set of instructions that computers may utilize to operate. They also work together to solve issues and run logic checks on their code as it runs through the system.

Nowadays, almost every company makes use of some sort of computer, and while the role of the computer programmer varies greatly depending on the sort of business for which he or she works. The position which is always taken into consideration owing to the great level of responsibility that is entailed as a professional. Computer programming has evolved significantly throughout the year's transformation as a result of technological advancement.

Programmers were at the front of this development of this transformation. At its core, computer programmers are tasked with informing computer systems on how to reflect by entering a set of data and algorithms and then making adjustments to those formulae when difficulties develop. Time and experience requirements for different forms of programming are different as well.

Simple programs may normally be built in a couple of hours. However, more complicated programs might take years to finish, depending on the complexity. In any case, the computer programmer must be fluent in the programming language and capable of solving issues "on the fly" via the use of logical reasoning and sequence. A bachelor's degree in computer science is necessary for most computer programming positions, according to one of the more popular career websites. However, some skilled programmers have learned and improved their abilities only through on-the-job training rather than through a formal education program. Because of the entry-level education criteria, most programmers are forced to explore new extensive training options to reregulate keep up with the newest technical advancements in their industry.

1.3 You Can Learn Computer Programming!

Programming is a skill that almost everyone can acquire. The conditions are few (like access to a computer), and you don't need to be a mastermind to be successful. It certainly helps if you're a genius, but you don't need to be one (although it helps). This chapter tackles some of the objectives you might want to learn how to program a computer, some things to consider, and explore a few different approaches to start studying right away! Read on! There are a variety of reasons why you would wish to study computer programming, and deciding what you want to achieve with it can help narrow down your options in choosing a learning path. Perhaps you are interested in pursuing a career in programming.

In that scenario, you'll want to make sure you're studying material that will make you more attractive to employers who are looking for programmers. As an alternative, you may be searching for an interesting pastime to pass the time, in which case you can be a little more casual about what you study and concentrate exclusively on topics that interest you. You may need to automate many programs you use at work. Examples include automating a word processor to create mailing labels or spreadsheets to make personal financial forecasts, as well as writing computer games and creating a beautiful Web site. The list of possible uses for computers is as vast as the list of things you can do with them. These considerations will have an impact on the programming languages you study, as well as the method you'll want to follow when you begin learning computer programming. Time, money, people who can help you, computers, books, programming clubs, courses, programming forums, and so on are all things that will help you learn to program. You're welcome to reach out to us with your quires. It's likely that if you have a lot of free time and money, a computer, and access to learning opportunities such as college courses and development group meetings, you will be able to acquire new skills very quickly. If you can only dedicate an hour or two per day, if you are unable to use a computer system, if all you can afford are a few books, you'll need to adapt to your expectations. However, you will be able to learn to program either way or anywhere in the middle of the spectrum. This is a very important point to consider.

It will not be easy to get through this. You have to keep going even when things seem tough, and you can't seem to find the answers you're looking for. Doing this requires a significant amount of mental energy, willpower, and the ability to sort things out. You'll do well if you can maintain a "stick-it-out" mindset throughout the process. One of the appeals of computer programming is that it involves a great deal of problem-solving, and problem-solving a lot of problems while you are learning and when you are applying your knowledge to relevant tasks, it will be difficult to sustain the interest and devotion long enough to achieve success; But, if it still sounds appealing to you, you should be able to accomplish your goals. A variety of approaches can be used to get started.

No matter how you want to handle it in the long term, you can start right away and work your way up from there. Here are some pointers to help you get started early: Learn little by little - Start with something simple and build on it slowly. Unless you have endless time and money, there's no use going in with both hands. The simplest way to get started may be to use a programming language that comes pre-installed with the tools you already have. For example, in Microsoft Word, you can do a great deal of programming using Visual Basic for Applications (VB for Applications). Many commercial software programs can be customized using programming or scripting languages , and this is becoming more common. Another suggestion for a faster start is as follows: The ability to automate repetitive operations is accessible with practically any operating system (Windows, Linux, and Mac) through the use of native scripting languages. For example, VBScript can be used with Windows to create scripts.

If you need more information, a simple online search will provide plenty of results. Choose a more comprehensive language that is also available for free. - For those who want to get started with the least amount of expense and as fast as possible, one option is to get a free programming environment from the Internet. For example, you can get the Ruby programming language and everything you need to get started with it for free. NET Express programming languages (for example, VB.NET or C# are ideal possibilities) are another example - once again, you can get everything you need from Microsoft for no cost. The information you want can be found by doing a simple Internet search on the words "Ruby Language" or "Microsoft.NET Express." Use the Internet - Even if you already know it, or you may not be reading this post, the Internet is full of tools to help you with your programming endeavors. This is logical, given that programmers were responsible for building and programming the Internet. There are a large number of programmers willing to contribute their expertise through free tutorials, forums, advice sites, and chapter presentations. If you do just one search, you will connect to a huge number of useful sites.

Whatever it is, there is no dearth of information for the public. Take your approach to what you have or what you can easily get - my advice to start fast is to do something right away and keep doing something every day. Soon, you will be able to better determine which subjects of study are most attractive to you and best meet your needs, as well as the knowledge you need to continue your studies. Is. Book resellers and private individuals form a network that allows many of the Internet's book merchants to provide secondhand books through a network of thousands of other book dealers and private individuals. This way you can save a lot of money.

Write simple programs to help you automate something that is currently taking up your time after you start. Example: If you back up the files you've worked on by copying "by hand" to a CD at the end of each day, you can develop software that automatically finds your working folders and copies the files for you - all without your involvement. Because of each little help program you create, you'll get valuable extra time that you can use to advance your programming knowledge. Search and join "user groups" for computer programmers in your area. Almost all major cities have clubs like this that meet regularly - usually once a month or more.

Many of these meetings are free, and most of them include how-to talks on doing various programming tasks in different programming languages. In addition, they often organize study groups and introductory classes. No matter how many languages are represented, something is better than nothing, so it may be a good idea to attend any gathering like this so you can find that it is within acceptable driving distance. Take beginners' courses at a local community college or extended study program to learn the basics. These lessons are usually offered at a very low rate, and they will help you get your business up and running. I discovered that many of these programs are available online, making it relatively simple to enroll in a course like this one if you're eligible. Programming can be enjoyable, difficult, helpful, and financially rewarding. Not everyone has the natural aptitude or inclination to pursue a career as a full-time programmer, but practically everyone who can operate a computer can learn to program to do something useful or enjoyable. If you think this would be something you would be interested in, I urge you to give it a try and see what it holds for you. It will take time and determination to become proficient, but it all starts with a step in the right direction. So now is the time to take action.

Chapter 2

Why Learn C ++?

This is a fundamental language in case those programs may be divided into parts and logical units, and it has a significant library that is supported and a large range of data types. It also includes a plethora of programming languages. A C ++ executable is an operating system but is not machine-independent (applications generated on Linux will not run on Windows), but it is machine-independent. It is classified as a mid-level language because it enables the computer to produce complete programming (drivers, kernels, networking, and so on) as well as a large number of user applications. Support for a large variety of libraries: This framework has library support. To facilitate rapid and rapid development, it provides significant support for (standard underlying data structures, algorithms, and so on) as well as for third-party libraries (e.g., the Boost library). C ++ programs do very well in terms of execution speed because it is a compiled language that is also quite procedural. Modern programming languages include more built-in default features, such as garbage collection, dynamic types, and other bottlenecking features—the overall execution of the program.

Due to the lack of extra processing cost, it is substantially quicker in C ++. C ++ has pointer support, which allows users to directly alter the storage address. This is helpful while conducting low-level coding (where one may need explicit control over the storage of variables). OOP: This is a key element of the language that distinguishes it from C. The object-oriented support in C ++ makes it simple to create maintainable and extendable programs. Large-scale uses, on the other hand, are feasible. Procedural programming gets increasingly difficult to maintain as the codebase grows in size. Because C ++ is a compiled language, it performs better overall. Because C ++ is so near to the hardware, it allows you to operate at a lower level, providing you more control over memory management, quicker performance, and, ultimately, more flexible software development.

C ++ is a great place to start if you want to learn object-oriented programming. The notion of low-level polymorphism implementation may be found while creating virtual table pointers, as well as when creating dynamic type identification. C ++ is an ecologically friendly programming language that thousands of computer programmers rely on worldwide. As a skilled C ++ coder, in no circumstances you'll run short of opportunities. You get well compensated for your efforts. C ++ programming is a popular programming language in the field of application development. In conclusion, you will become an expert in a certain field of software development. When you grasp C ++, you will be able to distinguish between linker, loader, and compiler, as well as various types of data, variables, and its scopes, storage classes. There are several grounds why you should learn C ++ programming. One thing is certain when it comes to studying any language, even C ++: you must practice coding over and over again until you become an expert in the meaning of the language. Practice is required.

2.1 Benefits of C ++

When it comes to programming languages, C ++ has been considered as a transitional programming language, which implies that it allows for High-standard application development as well as low-Standard library development that is near to the hardware. In the opinion of many programmers, C ++ is the best of both worlds: it is a high-level language that allows one to develop complex applications while also providing flexibility in that it allows the developer to extract the best performance possible through accurate control of resource consumption and availability.

Despite the advent of newer programming languages such as Java and others based on the.NET framework, C ++ has stayed relevant and has progressed as a programming language. Some programmers like the capabilities provided by newer languages, such as garbage collection, which is implemented as a runtime component and allows for better control of memory. Although this is the case, C ++ continues to be the programming language of choice for developers that want precise control over their application's resource consumption and performance. Most applications have an architecture with several layers, with a web server written in C ++ serving components written in HTML or Java or.NET as the backbone of the system. We can build code without having to worry about the hardware since C ++ has this property of portability built into it. Moving the development of software from one platform to another is made possible by this method. If, for example, you're working on a Windows operating system and need to move to a LINUX operating system for whatever reason, the operating system of Linux executes the codes of the windows operating system smoothly and without a hitch. It is possible to regard Java as both a Low-Level and High-Level programming language due to its mid-level classification.

Being a supreme language, its features assist in the game development as well as in desktop applications, whilst low-level language characteristics aid in the construction of kernels and drivers. C ++ provides the most benefits in OOP principles like (Polymorphism) (Encapsulation) (Inheritance) and (Abstraction) when compared to other computer languages. Because this functionality was not available in C at the time, it proved to be quite beneficial in allowing users to work with data is in the form of classes and objects. A paradigm is a strategy that goes into programming. It is concerned with logic, style, and how we achieve the program's objectives. DMA (Dynamic Memory Allocation) is a C ++ technology that allows you to easily free and allocate memory. Due to the lack of a garbage collection system in C ++, the programmer has total control over memory management.

We don't need to install any additional runtime components to run the application because C ++ is a Compiler Based programming language. And the outcome is pre-interpreted, allowing the code to be executed faster and with more power. Even compilation and execution times have been lowered, allowing for the creation of a diverse set of programs ranging from games to drivers to complicated graphical user interfaces. C ++'s syntax is comparable to that of C#, C, and Java. If you already know one of these languages, learning C ++ will be a breeze. As a result, switching between languages becomes easier. This has the extra benefit of being compatible with C applications, which means that any C program that is already running may be turned into a C ++ application. In most cases, we just need to run the application on a single file. CPP extension is employed. The C ++ has a plethora of installed libraries.

They help in accelerating the software design and in providing users with the opportunity to accomplish more with less. C ++ is useful for designing games as well as graphical user interfaces (GUI). C ++ is also great for creating real-time visual and algebraic simulations. As a result, C ++ is useful in all fields. C ++ has a huge and active community behind it. The scale of your company is vital if you wish to seek aid regularly. The wider the community, the more and more help you will get in resolving your issues. There are several paid and free online courses and seminars that explain how community assistance works.

As a result, resource-intensive applications can be developed using C ++, as programs can be written less and extensively. Knowing that C ++ offers advantages in a variety of fields from banking to app development, user interface design to video games, it is no surprise that C ++ has a huge job market. Working knowledge of C ++ can help you get employment in departments where C ++ is required. When it comes to pointers in C ++, understanding them is a particularly difficult idea compared to other topics. It is possible that uninitialized pointers can cause a system failure. Memory corruption can also occur if wrong values are entered in the memory location. Overall, pointer problems are very difficult to diagnose, which makes them one of the biggest drawbacks of the C ++ programming languages. Since C ++ does not have a garbage collector, the user is responsible for managing all the data in memory in his program. In its absence, duplicate data gets stored, and the amount of available memory increases in the widest sense. C ++ is intrinsically risky. The major source of these security problems is the usage of pointers, global variables, and other related constructions.

As a result, mistakenly accessing a block of memory may wreak havoc on a whole application. It is a multi-paradigm language, which means it supports OOP with runtime polymorphism, templates, and static polymorphism, as well as certain functional programming capabilities. C ++ is unsuitable for platform-dependent applications, and as a result, it gets difficult when employed in massive high-level software. When it comes to syntax, C ++ is rather strict, and even the tiniest mistake may cause a chain reaction of problems. C ++ takes the most time to master than any other programming language. As previously said, producing comprehensible C ++ code is challenging, making the language less friendly. Many programming languages, such as Java, enable us to create operators that execute specific data operations.

However, this is not entirely possible in C ++. We can utilize operator overloading to redefine existing operators, but we can't do much else. The C ++ programming language does not provide built-in threads. Even though this is a novel notion, it was eventually incorporated into the most recent edition of the C ++ standard. However, it is still a long way off when compared to languages like Java. Tuples and struts are two algebraic data types that C ++ does not support. As a result, if we need to use it, we'll have to rely on libraries or write our executables.

2.2 Why Should We Prefer C ++?

It is compatible with official (Object-Oriented) and (Generic Programming) languages. And they have a comprehensive Standard Library that includes a diverse range of functions for file handling as well as techniques for manipulating data structures simply and efficiently, among other things. This programming language is extensively used by programmers and developers, mostly in the application development industry. It comprises all of the essential components, including the core language, which provides all of the necessary building pieces, such as variables, data types, constants, and so on. When it comes to building programs, C ++ has a variety of applications and advantages. As an example, consider the apps that are built around the graphic user interface (GUI), such as Adobe Photoshop and others. It is popular among students as a first language to learn and is taught in many schools. Major software producers, sellers, and giants utilize C ++ to develop a variety of applications. For example, Google's Big Table, Google File System, Google Chromium web browser, and Map Reduce big cluster data processing are all developed in C ++. C ++ is also used to develop a variety of other applications. Mozilla makes use of a subset of the C ++ programming language. It is necessary to have C ++ 14 installed to build Mozilla

The Mozilla Firefox web browser and the Thunderbird email chat client are both developed in C ++. A large number of Windows applications that you use daily are written in C ++. This package contains tools for creating and debugging C ++ code, particularly code built for the DirectX, Windows API, and .NET frameworks. Rock star Games: C ++ is used by almost all major video game companies since it runs at a fast enough speed on bare metal.

Many large gaming engines are designed entirely in C ++, making use of the language's speed and object-oriented programming features. MongoDB is an open-source database that is extensively used as the back-end store for online applications, as well as in big organizations such as Viacom, biotechnology corporations, and Disney. It is also used as a front-end store for web applications.

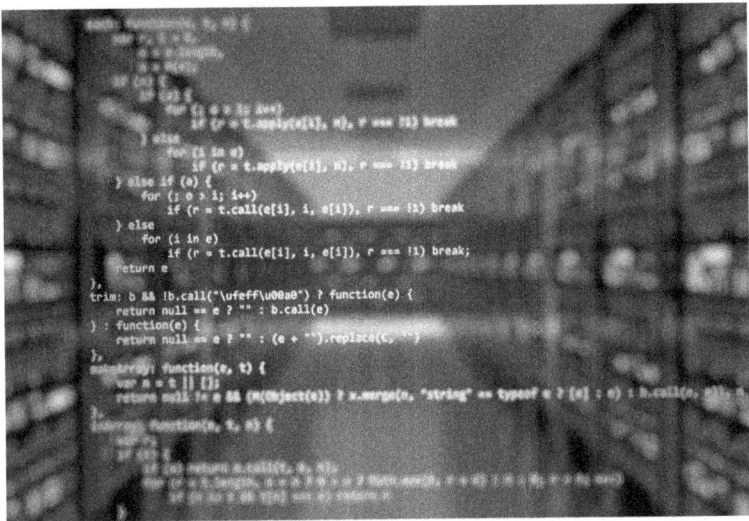

C ++ is a programming language that is used for game development. It reduces the complexity of three-dimensional games and aids in the optimization of available resources. With networking, the multiplayer option is supported in C ++. It is preferred because it is very quick in terms of runtime and since it's primarily used in the creation of gaming toolkits. It is frequently utilized in the development of actual (Image Processing) visual effects, and (Mobile Sensor) apps, as well as modeling, all of which are mostly developing in (C ++) programming languages. This program is used for a variety of tasks including animation, environment creation, motion graphics, and virtual reality. These virtual reality gadgets are the most well-known in today's modern creative industry, and they are also the most expensive.

C ++ is also used for a variety of media-related tasks such as developing a media player and handling video and audio data. Take, for example, the Win amp Media Player, which was designed in C ++ and enables users to listen to music while also accessing, sharing, and transferring movies and audio files, among other things. We are all familiar with how compiled languages work, which is one of the primary reasons why most compilers are built entirely in the C ++ programming language. The compilers compiled such as (C#) (Java) language and so on are almost entirely in(C ++) and also employed in the development of that kind of language since (C ++) is an independent platform and may be used for the production of a wide range of Software applications. Application programs such as film scanners and camera scanners are also written in the C ++ programming language. It has been employed in the development of PDF technology for print documentation, the exchange of documents, the publication of papers, and the archiving of documents, among other things.

Chapter 3

History of C ++

C++ editing language has a long and admirable history dating back to 1979 when Bjarne Stroustrup embarked on a career in his medical dissertation. One of the languages Stroustrup had, the Simula, provided an opportunity to collaborate on a programming language intended for computer simulation. The Simula 67 planning language, in which Stroustrup is involved, is often recognized as the first language to support an object-oriented planning paradigm, 1967. Even though Stroustrup found that this paradigm is very effective. In software development, the Simula programming language was too lazy to be used practically. His next project was "C with Classes," which aimed to be the superset of the C editing language. Suddenly he started working on it. They aimed to integrate programs that focused on the object in the C programming language, which was considered and continues to be respected for their effectiveness without compromising process speed or low-level skills. In addition to all the features of C language, classification, inlining input of native heritage, default parameters for operational calls, and solid test type are all included as features in their language.

Initially, there was a C facilitator with a class called Cfront, which came from another C facilitator called CPre. It was software designed to convert C into an old C code with class code. The fact that Cfront was highly developed by classes in C makes it a self-contained producer, more important to mention (a compiler that can integrate itself). Cfront would eventually be discontinued in 1993 because it seemed impossible to add new features, such as the C ++ variant, to the codebase. On the other hand, Cfront has been instrumental in the development of the latest developers and the Unix operating system. In 1983 the name of the editing language was changed from C to C ++ by Class. The ++ user in the C programming language is used for flexibility enhancement, which provides some information about how Stroustrup perceives language. This is also the time when several new features, most popular of which were visual functions, overload, and indexes using the symbol, const key, and single-line comments using two forward tails (a feature derived from the BCPL language), were introduced.

C ++ Programming Language, a language reference written by Stroustrup and released in 1985, was the first publication on the subject. C ++ was first released as a commercial product in the same year that it was launched. Since language was not officially banned, this book served as a very useful reference. The language was revised again in 1989, this time to add protected and standing members and a legacy from many categories, among other things. The Annotated C ++ Reference Manual, published in 1990, is a must-have for all C ++ program editors. The Turbo C ++ compiler developed by Borland will be launched as a commercial product next year. Turbo C ++ includes a few new libraries that will greatly contribute to the development of the C ++ editing language. Even though the latest and Stable Version of (Turbo C ++) was developed in 2006, When the C ++ Standards Committee issued (ISO / IEC 14882: 1998) to be officially called (C ++ 98), it was a momentous moment in the history of programming languages. The Annotated C ++ Reference Manual, according to some, has been instrumental in improving the quality of the spoken word. The Standard Template Library, whose conceptual development began in 1979 and came into use in 1980, was also included. After receiving several reports of difficulties with its 1998 standard, the committee responded by reviewing the standard in 2003 to address those issues. C ++ 03 was the name given to the new editing language. In 2005, C ++ Standards Group published a technical report (named TR1) outlining the various additions to the latest C

++ language version. The new standard was officially called C ++ 0x because it was to be distributed before the end of the first decade of the 21st century. Ironically, a new standard could not be announced until mid-2011, much to our surprise. Many technical books had been published before, and many compilers began to add support for the testing of new skills. The updated version of C ++ (named C ++ 11) was completed in mid-2011.

This new level is strongly influenced by the Boost library effort, and many new modules are developed directly from the same Boost library. New features include regular speech support (more information about common expressions can be found here), complete randomization library, new C ++ library, atomic support, general addiction library (i.e., since 2011, available at C and C ++). + both were lacking). New loop syntax that provides the same functionality for each loop in other languages, default keyword, new container classes, better union support, and program-initiated lists, and a new C ++ library.

3.1 Communication with C Programming

C ++ was first created in 1979 by Bjarne Stroustrup at Bell Labs to serve as a replacement for the C programming language. In contrast, C ++ was created as an object-oriented programming language that implements principles such as inheritance, abstraction, polymorphism, and encapsulation in addition to the more traditional C language. Classes are a feature of C ++ that are used to store and manage member data and member functions these member methods.

3.2 Evolution of C ++

Because of its widespread use, years of development have resulted in C ++ being accepted and embraced on a wide range of platforms, with the majority of them employing their C ++ compilers. Consequently, compiler-specific variations occurred, resulting in compatibility concerns as well as porting difficulties. As a result, there was a pressing need to standardize the language and give compiler makers a common language specification with which to operate. The ISO Committee approved the first standard version of C ++ in 1998, resulting in the publication of ISO/IEC 14882:1998. Since then, the standard has undergone significant revisions that have increased the usability of the language while also broadening the scope of the standard library's support. As of the date of publication of this book, the most recent approved version of the standard is ISO/IEC 14882:2014, sometimes known as C ++14 unofficially.

Chapter 4

Features, Uses
& Applications of C ++

It's a vast list of C ++-programmed programs, operating systems, online services, databases, and corporate software, to name a few examples. Whatever your profession or what you do with a computer, the odds are that you are already consuming software written in the C ++ programming language. In addition to software professionals, C ++ is often the language of choice for research work by physicists and mathematicians who are doing experiments in quantum mechanics. When you launch Notepad on Windows or the Terminal on Linux, you are instructing the CPU to execute an executable version of the application you are attempting to run. The executable is the completed result that can be executed and should accomplish the goals that the programmer set out to accomplish.

4.1 Uses of C ++ Programming Language

As previously said, C++ is among the highly adopted editing programs worldwide. Nearly every element of software development, including web development, uses it. A short list is presented in this section: Application software is developed using the C ++ program, many operating systems, such as Windows, Mac OSX, along with Linux IS, have utilized it in their development as well as the operating system, C ++ has been used to build key features for a number of internet browsers, together-with Google Chrome as-well-as Mozilla Firefox. C ++ was also used in the development of MySQL, the most widely used data system. Editing language evolution - C ++ has now been widely utilized in the development of the latest editing languages such as C #, JavaScript, Unix's-C-shell, Perl, PHP and Python, Java, and Verilog. Computational Programming – scientists consider C ++ as one of the most popular programming languages due to its speed and high computer performance. Game engine building - Because of the fast performance of C ++, it lets programmers create intensive CPU process processes and have better control over the hardware.

As a result, it is often used in the development of gaming engines. In the development of medical and engineering applications, such as MRI software, advanced CAD / CAM programs, and other similar programs, C ++ is widely used as an embedded system. The services of C ++ go on and on. At a number of places, software experts testify to be satisfied to produce the best software products using C ++. I highly recommend for you to understand and learn it so that you can make a significant contribution to the community through software development. After exploring C ++ skills, these are some of the interesting places where this language is often used. C ++ is used to configure all applications, including Microsoft Windows, Mac OS X, and Linux. Because it is the most typed and fast editing language, C / C ++ serves as the basis for all the most popular applications.

This is because it is an ideal choice for designing operating systems as they are solidly typed and fast. Additionally, C is similar to compound language, making it easier to write standard operating system modules in C. Due to the speed provided by C ++, the rendering engines of various web browsers are written in this programming language. Dedicated search engines require a quick launch to ensure that consumers do not have to wait for content to be displayed on the screen. As a result, C ++ is used as the programming language for these types of low-latency systems.

In a huge number of high-quality libraries, C ++ is the principal planning language. Many machine learning frames, for example, rely on C ++ as their backdrop language because of its speed. Tensor Flow, one of the most frequently used machine learning libraries, is developed in the C ++ editing language on the library's back end. Such libraries necessitate the usage of highly efficient computing resources since they reproduce enormous matrices for training machine learning techniques. As a response, performance is increasingly crucial. C ++ is useful when working with such libraries. All image programs must deliver quicker to be successful, and C ++, in the case of web browsers, aids in this endeavor by reducing latency.

The programming language of choice for all software that uses computer vision, digital image processing, or high-end graphics processing is the C ++ programming language. Even the most popular games with lots of visuals rely heavily on C ++ as their main programming language. As a result of the speed provided by C ++ in these scenarios, developers can reach a wider audience by optimizing their applications for low-end devices that do not have a lot of computing capacity. Infosys Finacle uses C ++ as one of its backend coding languages, a core-banking system that is one of the most widely used in the world. Banking applications handle millions of transactions every day and require support for high concurrency and low latency to function properly.

C ++ naturally becomes the programming language of choice in such applications due to its speed and multithreading capabilities. These functionalities are enabled by the numerous standard template libraries provided with the C ++ programming kit. Furthermore, huge organizations that are developing cloud storage systems and other distributed systems choose C ++ since it connects with hardware incredibly well and is compatible with a wide range of processors. Cloud storage solutions make use of scalable file systems that are proximate to the hardware on which the data is stored. C ++ becomes the superior language to deal with in such situations because it has hardware and because the multithreading libraries in C ++ provide higher concurrency and load tolerance, both of which are vital in such contexts. Databases such as Postgres and MySQL are written in the two most often used programming languages, C ++ and C, which is a forerunner of the C programming language. They are used to store and retrieve information in almost all of the well-known apps that we all use in our everyday lives, such as YouTube and Quora. C ++ is used as the primary programming language in a variety of embedded systems, including medical devices, smartwatches, and other wearable devices, since it is more intimately coupled to the hardware level than other high-level programming languages. Is.

C ++ is widely utilized in a variety of applications, including programming telephone switches, routers, and space probes since it is one of the quickest programming languages accessible. Compilers for different computer languages utilize as backend programming languages; C and C ++ are used. This is because C and C ++ are both low-level languages that are closer to hardware and, as a result, are an excellent fit for such compilation systems due to their low degree of abstraction. These are only a few examples of how the C ++ programming language may and should be utilized. In this part, you will learn more about the advantages of C ++ over other programming languages.

4.2 Features of C ++

The following are among the most intriguing characteristics of C++: It's a computer language focused on object-oriented programming. This implies that the emphasis is on "things" and the changes that take place around these objects. No information is provided to the consumer of the item as to how these operations are conducted because this information is abstract. A large number of functions are provided through the C ++ Standard Template Library (STL), which helps in the rapid development of code. Standard libraries for various containers, such as assets, maps, hash tables, and other similar constructs, are readily available. When latency is an important parameter, C ++ is the programming language of choice.

Most other general-purpose programming languages are extremely sluggish, both in terms of compilation and execution time. A C ++ application's compilation and execution times are relatively short. Unlike interpreted programming languages, which do not require compilation, C ++ code must be translated to low-level code before it can be executed. The C ++ programming language also features pointer support, which is commonly used in programming but is not necessarily accessible in other programming languages. Because nearly all of the programs and systems you use have some or all of their codebase written in C/C ++. As a result, it's now among the essential languages for programming and development. C ++ is included in almost all of the products we use daily, whether it is Windows, image editing software, your favorite game, or your web browser.

Here's a simple example of manipulating different features:

```cpp
#include<iostream>
#include<typeinfo>
int main()
{
        auto m_boolean = false;
        auto m_integer = 26;
        auto m_float = 26.24;
        auto pointer = &m_float;
        //Showing types of variables
        std::cout << typeid(m_boolean).name()
<< std::endl;
        std::cout << typeid(m_integer).name();
```

```
        return 0;
    }
```

4.3 Real-World Applications of C ++

C ++ is closer to hardware, allows simple resource manipulation, allows a technical program on CPU-intensive tasks, and it's too fast. In addition, this is capable of overcoming the complexity of (3D) Games and enabling multi-layer networks. The advantages of this language make the programming language of the first choice for building gaming systems and game development software packages. Since it has all the necessary functionalities, it would be used to create many graphical user interface desktop programs and GUI. The C ++ programming language is used to build most of the Adobe system's apps, such as Illustrator, Photoshop, and the like. Microsoft's Winamp Media Player is a well-known software that has been meeting all our music and video demands for decades.

The C ++ programming language was used to make this Software. Usage of c ++ in the development of Database administration applications. The most common databases are (MySQL) and (PostgreSQL), both of which are written in the C ++ computer language (Postgres). (MySQL) is a well-known database management system that is frequently used in real-world applications and is written in C ++. It is widely used as open sources Database in the world. Database, which was created in C ++, IS used by many companies. And the fact is that C ++ is a suitable choice for creating operating systems and apps because it is a strictly typed and fast language. As a bonus, C ++ offers a large system-level library of operations that can be used to write low-level applications. Some of the code in Apple's operating system OS X is developed in C ++. Similarly, components of both the iPods are written in C ++. Most of Microsoft software is written in (C ++) many Versions of (Visual C ++). Which is used for writing applications like (Windows 95) (ME, 98 (XP), and other operating systems. In addition, C ++ is used in the development of Integrated Development Environments (IDEs), Internet Explorer and Microsoft Office. Browser is mostly used in C ++ for rendering purposes. Since most users don't want for waiting for the loading of the web page, the rendering engine should be as quick as possible in terms of execution. Due to the high efficiency of C ++, the rendering software in most browsers is developed in C ++. Mozilla Web Browser is a free and open-source program.

Firefox is a free and open-source project written entirely in the C ++ programming language. Thunderbird, Mozilla's email client, is written in C ++ in the same way that the Firefox web browser is produced. This is a free and Open-Source application like the previous one. C ++ is used in developing Google programs such as the Google File System and the Chrome browser. For example, C ++ is beneficial in developing applications that demand image processing of high quality, actual physical simulation, and also portable sensor apps that must be both fast and perform well. It is built in C ++ and is used for animations (virtual reality), (3D graphics), and (environment). It is available through the alias system. As C ++ facilitates concurrency, it has become the programming language of selection for bank applications that require multi-threading, concurrent, and efficiency. Infosys Finacle is a very well banking services application with a backend written in C ++. Cloud storage solutions, which are becoming more popular, operate close to the hardware.

Because it is closer to that same hardware level, C ++ becomes the programming language chosen to build such systems. C ++ also has multithreading capabilities, which allow developers to create concurrent programs that are load tolerant. Bloomberg is a distributed relational database management system (RDBMS) designed to provide investors with reliable financial news and information in real-time While Bloomberg's Relational Database Management System (RDBMS) is developed in C, the company's C ++ is used to write the development platform and library set. Many high-level languages have compilers built in any C and C ++, based on the language.

Because both the programming languages are closely related to hardware and capable of programming and manipulating the underlying hardware resources, they are often used in embedded systems. C ++, in comparison to other high-level computer languages, is used to create a wide range of embedded devices such as smartwatches and medical device systems because it is closer to that same hardware level and has a large number of low-level can give function calls. (C ++) is used in the development of many commercial computer programs, along with complex applications like flight simulation & radar systems processing, are available. When conducting extremely complicated mathematical procedures, efficiency and performance become critical factors.

As a result, C ++ is the primary programming language used by most libraries. C ++ is the backend for the vast majority of a collection of high-level computer language libraries. C ++ is significantly quicker than other computer languages and, among other things, supports multithreading and concurrency. C ++ is also popular for constructing apps where speed and consistency are critical. C ++ is also closer to hardware, allowing us to manage hardware resources fast through the usage of low-level functions in the language. The result is that when it comes to applications that involve low-level manipulation and hardware programming, C ++ is the logical choice.

4.4 Where is C ++ used in industry?

C ++ has established itself as a programming language in practically everything. C ++ is the major programming language underlying numerous technical components, ranging from video games to databases to operating systems and everything in between. Its use in the actual world is so strong that, even after years of development and the introduction of several other enhanced languages, we cannot ignore its applications and benefits. C ++ is a programming language that is utilized in-game creation, like Sudoku, for example, which is one popular game many people across the world enjoy. Typically, it looks like this:

		1			3	9		2
	4			6	7	8		
			9		8			7
1		2						
5	9	8	6	2		7		
7		4	3				9	1
		7			9		8	6
9	1		8		6	3		4
6				4	2	1		

To code the game, follow as shown below:

```cpp
#include<iostream>
#include<vector>
#define MAX_NUMBER 9
Using namespace std;
bool checkSudokuBoard(vector<vector<int>>&);
int main() {
    vector< vector<int>> m_gameSudoku = {
        {5,3,0,0,7,0,0,0,0},
        {6,0,0,1,9,5,0,0,0},
        {0,9,8,0,0,0,0,6,0},
        {8,0,0,0,6,0,0,0,3},
        {4,0,0,8,0,3,0,0,1},
        {7,0,0,0,2,0,0,0,6},
        {0,6,0,0,0,0,2,8,0},
        {0,0,0,4,1,9,0,0,5},
        {0,0,0,0,8,0,0,7,9}
    };
    if (checkSudokuBoard(m_gameSudoku))
    cout << "Input Sudoko is valid\n";
    else
    cout << "Input Sudoko is not valid\n";
```

```cpp
        return 0;
}

bool
checkSudokuBoard(vector<std::vector<int>>&
_gameSudoku) {
        int numberCount[MAX_NUMBER];
        for (int horizontal = 0; horizontal <
MAX_NUMBER; ++horizontal) {
                memset(numberCount, 0, MAX_NUMBER
* sizeof(int));
                for (int vertical = 0; vertical <
MAX_NUMBER; ++vertical) {
                        if
(_gameSudoku[horizontal][vertical] != 0)

        ++numberCount[_gameSudoku[horizontal][
vertical] - '1'];
                }
                for (int i=0;i<MAX_NUMBER;++i)
                        if (numberCount[i] > 1)
                                return false;
        }
        for (int vertical = 0; vertical <
MAX_NUMBER; ++vertical) {
                memset(numberCount, 0, MAX_NUMBER
* sizeof(int));
                for (int horizontal = 0;
horizontal < MAX_NUMBER; ++horizontal) {
                        if
(_gameSudoku[horizontal][vertical] != 0)

        ++numberCount[_gameSudoku[horizontal][
vertical] - '1'];
                }
                for (int i=0;i<MAX_NUMBER;++i)
```

```
                if(numberCount[i]>1)
                    return false;
        }
        int block_hoizontal = 0,
    block_vertical = 0;
        for (int block = 0; block <
    MAX_NUMBER; ++block) {
            block_hoizontal = (block / 3) *
    3, block_vertical = (block % 3) * 3;
            memset(numberCount, 0, MAX_NUMBER
    * sizeof(int));
            for (int horizontal =
    block_hoizontal; horizontal <
    (block_hoizontal + 3); ++horizontal)
                for (int vertical =
    block_vertical; vertical < (block_vertical +
    3); ++vertical)
                    if
    (_gameSudoku[horizontal][vertical] != 0)

        ++numberCount[_gameSudoku[horizontal][
    vertical] - '1'];
            for (int i=0;i<MAX_NUMBER;++i)
                if (numberCount[i] > 1)
                    return false;
        }
        return true;
    }
```

As all of the numbers inside of a Sudoku game follow a valid pattern, the output will reign true.

C ++ is also the preferred programming language for designing banking applications, and many financial institutions are already using C ++ as their back-end programming language for development. The Finacle, developed by Infosys, is the greatest example of this. It is a well-known program that is utilized for financial purposes at Infosys. It is built on the C ++ programming language as its foundation. Concurrency, multithreading, speed, and high performance are all required by banking applications. All of these are important characteristics of the C ++ programming language! You may have been unaware of the real technology that is employed in the construction of scanners until now! Allow me to share it with you right now! The camera scanners and film scanners are controlled by the C ++ programming language.

They are mostly used in the technologies that facilitate the creation of PDF documents. These programs are used for a variety of tasks, including document creation, printing, and publishing. All of this is made possible through C ++! Aside from that, C ++ is also employed in the development of certain open-source and commonly used database software. MySQL, Postgres, and Bloomberg RDBMS are three of the most well-known database management systems, all of which were designed in C ++. Quora, YouTube, and other similar sites make considerable use of them. In practically all businesses, MySQL is commonly used open-source database software that is free to download and use. It aids in the saving of time, bundled software, money, and business processes, among other things. This database software was developed with pride in the C ++ programming language! The amount of data accessible is expanding as the number of people who have access to the Internet grows across the globe. Large enterprises rely on cloud computing and want solutions that are as near to the hardware as possible. C ++ is the most popular computer language for this purpose.

In practically every industry, C ++ is utilized, and here are the key reasons why C ++ is the most helpful and generally recognized programming language for producing apps, software, and other types of projects. It's the most popular computer language in the world. Many areas, such as gaming, websites, and other online services, place a high value on speed. You cannot legitimately wait for the back-end code to complete its execution while you wait for it to complete its execution. As a result, speed is a critical consideration while designing games, web servers, database systems, and other applications in C ++, among other things.

This language contains abstraction at a very low level. Consequently, it is more closely associated with hardware than any other programming language. The fact that it handles resources well means that it is always the recommended language to employ in areas where proximity to hardware is essential! As a result, we now understand how C ++ is useful in real life and why it is C ++ and not any other programming language that is as beneficial as it is! C ++ is a programming language that is utilized by numerous businesses and organizations.

Chapter 5

Top Reasons to Learn C ++

C ++ is of great importance today. There are many, like operating systems, web browsers, and other similar applications, all are contemporary systems, incorporating C ++ code into at least some part of their codebase. Furthermore, because of its speed, C ++ is very advantageous in areas where performance is critical. C ++ is the backbone of many advanced programming languages, including Java and Python. Regardless of whether the programming language is Java, Python, JavaScript, or any other, all of them are executed using C or C ++ as their execution engine.

Knowing just the syntax and libraries of a programming language will not help you become a competent programmer in that language. You must be familiar with the fundamentals of everything, which is the one and only C ++! Since the most obvious virtue of C ++ is that it is very scalable, it is often used to develop resource-intensive applications. Graphics use a significant amount of system resources, which is why the most beautiful 3D games you can find are typically designed using C ++, as is the case with most of the games you like playing. Whatever you are talking about, whether it is operating systems, internet browsers, or apps, C ++ is all around you. Google searches for the languages used for operating system foundation portions will reveal that Windows, Linux, Android, and even Mac/iOS are all built in the C programming language, as will other operating systems.

C ++ is used to create all of the popular internet browsers, such as Chrome, Firefox, and Safari. Additionally, if you are a gamer, you will be surprised to learn that C ++ is utilized to develop numerous gaming engines that are of a high degree of sophistication. The C ++ programming language is very fast and efficient. Of course, there are a plethora of languages that are more performing than C ++, but when utilized properly, the C ++ language may be even faster than Java! As previously said, since you have complete control over the resources utilized, large corporations rely on C ++ when they need to achieve faster performance with fewer resources than they have. If you are working with the C ++ programming language, you will quickly notice that interfaces are well specified and standardized in the C ++ programming language.

This suggests that it may be used by any sophisticated programming language since it can be used with a variety of compilers or different versions when writing and assembling it. In today's fast-paced world, high-performance apps are essential to be successful. If you are a developer, you may be following industry-best practices while implementing various solutions that are capable of performing effectively. In any case, knowing C ++ will assist you in gaining a better understanding of the performances.

You'll be capable of figuring out what's causing the problem and enhancing the overall performance of the application. Because C ++ has STL (Standard Template Library), it is incredibly helpful because it allows programmers to write code more rapidly when the situation calls for it. This library is divided into four main sections: functions, iterators, algorithms, and containers. Several databases make use of C ++. Its examples include MongoDB, MySQL, and a slew of others. The reason for this is that C ++ is a relatively contemporary programming language that supports features such as lambda expressions, exceptions, and so on.

Databases created in C ++ are utilized by practically all modern-day applications, including Twitter, YouTube, WordPress, and others. To create complex games, you must learn the language and programming tactics first. Numerous adaptable mobile games have been made with the game engines written in C ++. Larger firms, such as Facebook and Google, may also want C ++ engineers to assist them in optimizing their apps or working on their products, and you might make a substantial amount of money in this capacity.

5.1 C ++ Popularity and High Salary

It is the world's best frequently used programming language. Over 4.4 million developers use it all over the world. Furthermore, C ++ Developers are in high demand, they have some of the high-paid occupations in the market, and an average annual base income of $103, 036.

5.2 C ++ in Databases

MySQL, MongoDB, MySQL, and many other current databases have been developed in the C ++ programming language. This is because C ++ is relatively current and offers features such as Lambda Expressions etc. a large no of a database built into C ++ that are used in practically all the apps we use now, including Facebook, YouTube, and other social media platforms. How does it work? Well you must first create a connection handle structure:

```
MYSQL *mysql_init(MYSQL *);
```

Now create new sql connection:

```
MYSQL mysqlConnect(
    MYSQL con,
    const char *acc,
    const char *un,
    const char *pwd,
    const char *dbName,
    unsigned int p,
    const char *socket,
    unsigned int flgs
);
```

Now run SQL:

```
int mysql_query(MYSQL *connection, const
char *query);
error handle :
unsigned int mysql_err(MYSQL *conn);
char *mysql_error(MYSQL *conn);
```

5.3 C ++ in Web Browsers

The CGI (Cyber-Initiative) programming is a way to have your website do more for you. Keeping this in mind before going forward with the process, make sure that:

1) Your Web Server supports running programs from an outside source and it's been configured correctly so as not restrict what can be done on our end

2) You've got space limitlessly set aside where all these new additions will go - aka "The Cgi Directory"

```
<Directory "/var/www/cgi-bin">
    AllowOverride None
    Options ExecCGI
    Order allow,deny
    Allow from all
</Directory>

<Directory "/var/www/cgi-bin">
    Options All
</Directory>
```

5.4 C ++ in Embedded Systems

Because it is close to the level of hardware than other programming languages, it works especially well in embedded systems where all hardware & software are tightly connected. Here are rare embedded C ++ applications, including smartwatches, MP3 players, GPS programs, and other similar devices. Try to avoid using certain features when you can use explicit conversions instead.

For example:

```
class myClass;
myClass *ptr =
reinterpret_cast<myClass*>(0xfeaa);
```

5.5 C ++ in Operating Systems

Windows, Linux, Android, Ubuntu, and iOS are just a few operating systems created with an arrangement of both windows apps are built with C ++, but android apps built in java and C / C ++, with non-default C ++ support times, as is the case with Windows applications. Additionally, C ++ can be used to build the core of iPhone and iPad apps. Typically, both are in applications, and the reason is Speed and strictly typing of features of the programming language.

As an example, here's the coding to threading a program for Linux:

```
#include <thread>
void thread_entry(int foo, int bar)
{
    int result = foo + bar;
    // Do something with that, I guess
}
// Elsewhere in some part of the galaxy
std::thread thread(thread_entry, 5, 10);
// And probably
thread.detach();
// Or
std::thread(thread_entry).detach();
```

5.6 C ++ in Graphics

Due to the fast C ++ speed, it is often used in image-focused programs like (Image Processing, Computer Vision and Screen Recording Programs,) and more. This may include various games in which visuals play an important role in the overall structure.

Here's a simple start to a C ++ program that will read from the camera and display RGB images:

```
#include              <iostream>
#include "opencv2/opencv.hpp"

using namespace cv;

int main() {

VideoCapture camera(0);
if(!camera.isOpened()){

}
namedWindow("Camera Window");
while(true){
}

return 0;
```

5.7 C ++ has Abundant Library Support

The (Standard Template Library) in C ++ is much important as it allows programmers to write compact and fast code when the situation requires it. It consists of four components, namely (algorithms), (containers), (functions), and also iterator, among others—so many types of algorithms, like searching, filtering, and

58

so on. Classes using a variety of data structures, including stack, Rows, Hash Tables, Vector, Set, List, and Map, are stored in the container data building store. Factors are functions that cause the function of related functions, which would be changed with the given parameters. In addition, the iterator is used to deal with price sequences.

5.8 C ++ is Portable

All Programs written in C ++ can be transferred from one place to another without difficulty. It is the core reason why C ++ is often used in programs that require the development of a few platforms or devices. To make your code more portable across different platforms, you should use STL types when possible.

Be careful about using system dependent or APIs like UINT64 and DWORD on Windows because they might not work as expected there. If writing GUIs is necessary then try using a cross-platform toolkit such as Qt which provides support for many languages including C/C ++ alongside their own framework.

Something such as this:

```
#ifdef _WIN32
#include <windows.h>
#else
#include <unistd.h>
#endif
```

Chapter 6

Understanding of Complier & Types of Errors

In this chapter, we will learn about the working of compilers and different types of errors.

6.1 Learn About Compiler

Compilers use software that understands the code. Converts statements expressed in a specific programming language into machine code or "code," which is a language recognized and used by a computer processor. The editor can usually add one line at a time to the editor to produce statements of language in editing language like (Pascal or C). These are the source statements that will be included in the newly created file. The editor then introduces the appropriate language conjunction, conveying it as a file naming parameter containing source statements. During operation, the compiler analyzes (or analyzes) all the language statements before creating an exit code in a series of subsequent sections or "passing," which ensures that statements referring to other statements are correctly identified in the final output code. Object code or, in some cases, an object module is traditionally used to describe the output of the merging process (see below). (It should be emphasized that the word "object" is not related to an object-focused program in this context.) Because the object code is a machine code, it can only be processed by one processor at a time.

A sample C ++ source code performs the exact Approach. as this piece of work, but with more readability and flexibility:

```
int int_1, int_2, total_sum_of_numbers;
cin >> int_1;
cin >> int_2;
total_sum_of_numbers = int_1 + int_2;
cout << total_sum_of_numbers << endl;
```

A new feature of java, which is used in Object-focused programs, is the ability for compiling output which is known as (byte code), that can work in any computer network platform on which the (Jvm) or byte code is installed. The translator is available for translating byte code which would be made by a real hardware processor. Due to the use of this virtual machine, it is possible to compile and separate the byte code on the platform using a timely compiler. (Java Translator and Java Compiler also available.) Where more than one object module was to be used, and the sequence of commands or data for each object module to the instructions or data of another object module, some operating systems require additional action after integration: related location for instructions and data.

The output of the function was known as the load module, and the process is also known as coordinate planning. The compiler is used to work with 3GL and high-quality languages, sometimes used interchangeably. Compiler editor which works with programs written in the compiler language of the processor. When a piece of source code is created in a standard language such as Java, the compiler is used to convert the source code into a specific architecture of computer (For example, the Intel Pentium design).

Each time it is utilised, the resulting machine code can be applied against a individual set of data. Interpreters are provided with usable resource programs written in high-quality programming language and program data and then use the system as opposed to data to produce a variety of results. Unix shell translator, for example, allows users to interact with the operating system using commands. Remember that, like any other system, Interpreters and editors are written in a high-level programming language (It may or may not be the same as the language they received) which is subsequently translated into the machine instructions. Java translator, for instance, may be written in full C or Java if needed.

Because it does not generate Machine Language and does not decrypt the static code, it sometimes is known as a disrespectful machine. (It's critical to distinguish between constructing and translating into machine code. Since it repeatedly checks and analyses all statements in the system when the statement is tested in the process being processed, the translator is usually slower than- each step of the loop body. Numerous computer scripts, for instance, Lisp and Java, come along with translator as well as compiler. Java compiler, encoded in C, converts Java source programs (Java sections with java suffixes Java translator files (with .class extension). Java translator, also known as The Java-Virtual-Machine can transform bytes instructions into machine code either immediately or dynamically. and use that machine code (JIT: just a combination of time).

6.2 Major Steps of Compiler Execution

A software that directly converts pre-programmed script to machine code is known as Compiler. Such as "stainless steel" computer software and a readable computer. Computers are used in a variety of computer programs, including personal computers and embedded systems. The high-quality source code of the program developer written in the standard programming language is translated into the low-level object code by the developer, which allows the output to be "processed" by the processor. The resulting object code or, in some cases, the object module is officially named as the result of the merging process.

Compiling a program is the process of converting it from human-readable languages, like C or Java, into something that can be understood by your computer's Central Processing Unit (CPU).

When you execute this command, anything written in cpp will become a machine code that pertains only to CPUs; thus making them efficient at executing instructions quickly without any delay due to their complexity:

```
g++ -Wall -ansi -o prog prog.cpp
```

In order to create executable files from source code, you must perform the following four key steps:

1. The first is the preprocessor, which deals with headers and macros in your program's C ++ input file

2. The expanded source code for C ++ made by the processor

3. The compiler generates object-code that is further assembled for the device.

4. Compiler then takes the rough outline of your program and creates an interactive assembly language that you can use to develop a complete working system.

6.3 Analysis of Semantic Structure

This step is made up of several smaller stages in between. To begin, the structure of tokens, as well as their sequence about the grammar of a specific language, is scrutinized for accuracy. In the end, the parser and analyzer understand the meaning of the token structure to form an intermediate code, referred to as object code. When a relevant token is found in the program, the object code contains instructions that specify the processor action that should be taken. Last but not least, the complete code is analyzed and analyzed to determine if any optimizations are available. As soon as optimizations can be carried out, the required updated tokens are put into the object code to produce the final object code, which is then stored in a file with the appropriate name.

6.4 Error in C ++

An error is defined as an unauthorized activity made by the user that results in the software not functioning properly. Programming problems often go undiscovered until the software is compiled or run for the first time. Some of the faults prevent the application from being built or run. Others are harmless. Also, before the compilation and execution of the program, one must fix the errors. Preceding are by far the most frequently seen errors in a broad sense. By using this code below, you can flag the complier to stop preprocessing:

```
g++ -E prog.cpp
```

6.5 Syntax Errors

Grammar rules exist in computer languages, just as they do in human languages. Unlike humans, who are willing to communicate effectively even if their language isn't faultless, computers are unable to ignore flaws such as syntax errors. And let us take an example the right print syntax is anything is print ('hi'), and we make the mistake of forgetting one of the (parentheses) throughout the coding process. The error of syntax will occur, and the application will be unable to continue operating as a result. As your knowledge of the programming language grows, the likelihood of making syntax mistakes decreases. The simplest method to keep them from causing you difficulties is to become aware of them as soon as possible. Many text editors and integrated development environments (IDEs) will have the ability to notify you about syntax problems while you are writing. With the example below, we'll see what error, and outcome, would occur without putting a semicolon after a line:

```
#include<stdio.h>
int main()
{
        printf("First Program")
}
```

Output of program

```
Error: expected ';' before '}' token
```

6.6 Logical Error

Mistakes are very hard to detect in the mind. It all seems to work VERY well; you just stopped the computer from performing the wrong action. While the system sounds psychological, the output may not be what you expected. If you have not read the requirements properly before and wrote the code that returned the oldest user to your system when requesting the most current user in your system, you will make a serious mistake. Among the best-known examples is the 1999 NASA spacecraft disaster, which was caused by translation errors between English and American units. The program was written in one way. However, it had to work in another language. When you have finished doing your tests, show them to the product manager or product owner to get their approval for the idea you are going to write. Someone with extensive knowledge of the firm would have noticed that you do not specify that a new user is required in the example above. Check the example below:

```
#include<stdio.h>
int main() {
      for (int n=0;n<5;n++);
      {
            printf("First Program");
      }
}
```

OUTPUT:

Line only printed one time instead of 5 times.

6.7 Compilation Errors

The integration process is required for some programming languages. Your advanced programming language is transformed into a standard language that the machine can easily understand during integration. If the producer does not understand how to change your code to a lower-level code, this results in an integration error, which is called an integration time error. While trying to create a print ('hi,' the producer stopped and told us not to do it) after '. If you have an error in compiling time on your software, you will not be able to test or run it. You will find great benefits in avoiding these mistakes with information, but in general, a big part of what you can do is get a quick response when it happens. Some common compilation errors include:

Undeclared identifier : DayofYear.cpp : In function `int main()': DayofYear.cpp:25: `DayOfYear' undeclared(first use this function)

Meaning that variable[DayofYear] is trying to be pushed through before declaration.

Undeclared: abc.cpp : In function `int main()': abc.cpp:4: `cout' undeclared(first use this function)

This happens if you forget to include iostream.

Parse Error : somefile.cpp : 12 : parse error before `nothing'

This happens when a semi - colon isn't in place at the end of a previous command.

6.8 Runtime Errors

When a user tries to use your software, operating time errors arise. Although the code may work successfully on your machine, it may not work properly on a web server due to a different set or because it interacts with it in a way that causes a runtime error on the website. This means that if the form is submitted without a first word, your system will fail because it will try to capitalize the first letter of the word using something like params [: first name]. Capitalize.

```
// Example for run-time error in C ++
program
#include <iostream>
void main()
{
        int number = 8, divide = 0;
        //number is diveded by zero to program
will crash
        divide = number / 0;

        std::cout << "Answer = " << divide;
}
```

These errors occur while the system is running and may prevent the user from performing the tasks for which he or she is accountable. Keep reporting the best bugs to catch any running time issues and automatically unlock new news on your ticketing system as they arise. Try to gather some useful information in each issue so that you do not repeat the same mistake the next time. Using the frameworks and code stored by the community is an excellent way to reduce the risk of these types of emerging errors as the code is used in many different projects and thus meets and handles a large number of problems.

6.9 Arithmetic Errors

An arithmetic error is a type of error that involves both mathematics and logical thinking. For example, while solving a separation problem, you may find that you cannot split zero without encountering an error. People don't usually write 5/0, but you may not know that the size of anything in your system can sometimes be zero, which leads to this kind of error. If age, Ax, or all years have been zero, years of operation may produce the error. As established earlier, mathematical errors can lead to logical errors or, in the case of zero divisions, make a logical error. May cause work time errors. Having an inspection system that always includes cases such as zero or negative numbers is a good way to stop these arithmetic errors in their tracks. For example:

```
int square_of_number(int num)
{
        return num * num;
}
```

```
void func()
{
    checked
    {
        int output = square_of_number(2);
    }
}
```

Since there is not a run-time flag, it cannot control the overflow.

6.10 Resource Errors

The system on which your software is running will allocate a specific quantity of resources to the program's functioning. If anything in your code causes the computer to try to allocate more resources than it has available, a resource error may be triggered. If you made the mistake of building a loop that your code couldn't escape from, you'd quickly run out of resources. The while loop in this example will continue to add new members to an array as long as the loop is running. You will ultimately run out of memory. Unfortunately, resource problems may be difficult to find down because the machine on which you're working is usually of higher quality than the servers on which your code is running. Aside from that, simulating real-world use from a local computer is tough. Below are a couple of examples of resource errors you might come across:

Undefined keyword or key name: MFT_STRING

Receiving this error usually means that there may have been typos included in the definition of the resource.

String not found in DLGINCLUDE statement

That error means the statement did not specifically recognize a valid include file. Therefore, it has to use this syntax: filename.h

6.11 Interface Errors

In the case of interaction failure, there is a difference between how your product should be used and how it should be used. Most software components adhere to the standards. If the input you receive does not meet the conditions, your system may have a problem interacting. For example, if you have an API that requires certain parameters to be assigned and those parameters are not specified, an interaction error may occur. If the interface problems are not handled correctly, they will appear to be wrong at the end while they are wrong at the end of the caller. As a result, both parties may be disappointed. The most effective way to say this is to have some documentation and diagnose these issues so that you can effectively address the issue. "Hey, you have not provided us with the information we need to fulfill this request what he should do. It is possible that if you do not detect these problems and return them to the caller, they will appear as operating time errors in your report, and you will end up being more protective.

Here's an example:

```
class MyInterface{
public:
    virtual ~MyInterface(){}
    virtual void initialize() = 0;
```

```
    virtual void newValueSound(int stream,
double value) = 0;
    virtual void newValueAlg1(int stream,
double value) = 0;
    virtual void newValueAlg2(int stream,
double value) = 0;
};
When using this header for the interface

#include "MyInterface.h"

void someMethod(){
    MyInterface *interface;
}
```

One might come across this error:

```
error C2332: 'struct' : missing tag name
error C2011: '<unnamed-tag>' : 'enum' type
redefinition
error C2226: syntax error : unexpected type
'<unnamed-tag>'
```

Chapter 7

Fundamentals of C ++

No programming language is completely faultless. The good news is that a computer language is not perfect to be a helpful apparatus for developing good systems. A general-purpose programming language will never be ideal for all of the numerous jobs to which it will be used. Because excellence in one field implies specialization in another, what is excellent for one job is sometimes severely faulty for another. As a result, C ++ was created to be a useful tool for developing a broad range of systems and for expressing a wide range of concepts in a straightforward manner. The built-in elements of a language are not always sufficient to convey all that needs to be communicated. It isn't even the best-case scenario.

There are language features that are designed to accommodate a wide range of programming styles and methodologies. For this reason, it is important to concentrate on mastering the native and natural styles of a language rather than on memorizing every single detail of every linguistic aspect while learning a new language.

The ability to write programs is required; nevertheless, comprehending a programming language is more than simply an academic exercise. It is vital to put ideas into action in the real world. There is no benefit in learning the most esoteric language features or in using the greatest amount of language features when it comes to actual programming. It is of little interest to study a single linguistic characteristic in isolation. The feature only becomes meaningful and interesting when it is placed in the context supplied by the approaches and other features. To make sense of the next chapters, remember that the true goal of learning about C ++ is to be able to utilize language features and library capabilities in concert to enable effective programming styles within the framework of sound designs. There is no important system that is constructed only based on the linguistic characteristics that are used. We create and utilize libraries to make the work of programming easier while also improving the overall quality of our systems. Libraries are used to increase the maintainability, portability, and performance of the software.

Classes, templates, and class hierarchies are all examples of abstractions that are used to represent fundamental application notions in libraries. The standard library contains representations of many of the most basic programming concepts and ideas. As a result, knowing the C ++ standard library is an essential element of learning the language. When it comes to knowing how to use C ++ properly, the standard library is the storehouse for a lot of hard-earned information. C ++ is a programming language that is extensively used in education and research. Some people have been startled by this, pointing out that C ++ is neither the smallest nor most tidily written language of programming ever created, which is right. It is, however, as follows: It is sufficiently clean to be used effectively in the teaching of fundamental design and programming ideas.

A sufficient amount of detail is provided to allow for the teaching of advanced ideas and approaches. For tough tasks, this approach is sufficiently realistic, economical, and versatile. It is sufficiently commercial to serve as a vehicle for applying what has been learned to nonacademic use. Organizations and partnerships that depend on a variety of development and execution environments will have enough resources available. This language enables you to grow your skills over time. The most crucial thing to remember is while we learn (C ++) is to keep our attention on important concepts (like type security and resource management) techniques (like Resource management through the use of object scope and an iterator in the algorithm) rather than getting bogged down in language-specific nuances. A programming language's primary goal is to help you become a better programmer, which means that you'll be more successful at creating and implementing new systems, as well as maintaining existing ones. In this case, an understanding of design and implementation concepts is far more important than a thorough comprehension of all of the intricacies of the program. The ability to comprehend technical subtleties develops with time and with experience is built on rigorous checking of the static type, and the majority of approaches are aimed at obtaining a high degree of direct representing and abstracting of the programmer's ideas as effectively as possible. When compared to lower-level approaches, this can generally be accomplished without negatively impacting run-time and space economy. Programmers who are transitioning from another language to C ++ must acquire and internalize the idiomatic C ++ programming style and method to reap the advantages of the language. The same is true for programmers who are used to working with previous and less expressive versions of C ++.

When approaches that are useful in one language are applied carelessly to another, the result is generally clunky, poorly performing, and difficult to maintain code. In addition, writing such code may be very unpleasant since every line of code and every compiler error message serves as a constant reminder to the programmer that the language being used is not the same as "the old language." it may have been written in the manner of (Fortran), (C), (Lisp), Java, and other programming languages in any language; but, doing so in a language with a different philosophy is neither enjoyable nor efficient. Every language has the potential to be a rich source of inspiration for programmers writing C ++ applications. However, to be successful in C ++, concepts must be translated into something compatible with the overall structure and type system of the programming language. Only Pyrrhic wins are conceivable while battling against a language's fundamental type structure.

In the ongoing discussion over whether or not one should study C before moving on to C ++, I am adamant that it is preferable to skip C and get right into C ++. Using C ++ instead of C minimizes the need to concentrate on low-level approaches and makes them safer and more expressive. After you have been introduced to the common subset of C and C ++, as well as some of the higher-level methods available directly in C ++, you will find it simpler to understand the difficult sections of C that are required to compensate for the language's lack of higher-level features.

7.1 Learning C ++

In this post, I will introduce you to the foundations of the C ++ programming language, starting with the most basic concepts. I'll go over all of the fundamentals you'll need to know before getting started with the C ++ programming language in this section. To guide you through the fundamentals of the C ++ programming language, I'll start by writing a very simple hello world program and then proceed to educate you through all the key essentials of C ++ language step by step, beginning with the most fundamental concepts. So let's begin by building a very basic hello world program to get things started. # Contains the standard C++ header file's contents, iostream via the use of a preprocessor directive known as "include." iostream is a header file included with the standard library that defines both in-put and out-put streams.

It's included in the library's standard distribution. These definitions are contained inside the STD namespace, which will be discussed further below. Programs can receive input and output from an external system – often the terminal – using standard input/output (I / O) streams. Main () is a new function that is defined by the int main () function. During the program's execution, the main function is invoked as a matter of convention. In a C ++ program, there should only be one main function, and it should return several types of INT unless otherwise specified. The INT in this case represents what is referred to as the return-type function. The main function returns a code indicating that the program has terminated. A system that is executing the software considers an EXIT SUCCESS or exit code of 0 to be a success, according to a convention. Any other return code indicates that an error has occurred.

If there is no return statement in the program, by-default, the primary function (by extension, the entire script) returns 0. Such approach does not require us to enter return 0 explicitly. Other than those that return null, all other functions must either clearly return the value aligned with the return-type or fail to return anything. This example writes "Hello World!" to the standard output stream using the function STD::cout "Hello World!" we have two distinct types of scope resolution operators in a namespace, and the first is the scope resolution operator that enables you to search up items in a namespace by their names. There are a plethora of namespaces. We use the prefix: to indicate that we wish to utilize the count function from the STD namespace. The iostream library refers to this object as the (STDout). It prints to the output device. Throughout this scenario, the operator for stream insertion is denoted by the symbol, which is so named because it adds an item into the object of the stream. The insertion of data into output streams is defined by the operator in the standard library, which may be used for certain data types. Stream content is a function that inserts material into a stream and returns the same stream with the content updated. Stream insertions may now be chained together as follows: This example outputs "FooBar" to the console using the STD::cout function. In computing, a character string literal, often known as a "text literal," is defined as "Hello World!" The iostream file contains the definition of the character string literal stream insertion operator. When you use this "STD::endl", it will insert the end-of-line characters and then flush the stream buffer, causing the text to appear correctly on the terminal. Using this method, you can be certain that the data you put into the stream will display on your terminal. Most of the time, a compiler generates the executable computer code for the C ++ language.

A compiler is software that converts code written in one computer language into a different format that is (more) directly executable by a computer, known as a machine translation. Compilation refers to the process of converting code using a compiler. C++ shares the C compilation process's structure, which is considered to be its "father" language. Compilation in C ++ is broken down into four major phases, which are detailed below. The C++ preprocessor mimics the data of all header files contained in the script file, generates macro code, and replaces symbolized values stated with the #define command with their contents, as specified. Using the C ++ preprocessor, you may create source code files that are ready to be translated further into the target network's assembly language.

It's necessary to assemble the assembly code produced by the compiler into object code that is suitable for the platform in question. A link is created between the object code file produced by the assembler and the computer code files for all library functions that were used to generate a workable file. Many C ++ compilers additionally include the ability to combine or unmerge portions of the compilation process for the sake of convenience or further examination. Even while many C ++ programmers may utilize a variety of tools, all of these tools will typically follow the same overall procedure when it comes to creating a program. So those were the key concepts that you needed to understand before getting started with the C ++ programming language. It was created as an extension to the C language. The addition of tools for profane programming, as well as the expansion of the standard library, were the two most significant new features. C ++ is a language that is utilized in several applications nowadays. It is still helpful for certain applications, like game development, even if it has been partially displaced on Windows PCs by.NET programming.

7.2 Standard Template Library

Stl has container classes, which have the purpose of containing other objects. The classes that are included are list, vector, multi-set, multimap, map, hash_set, hash_multiset, hash_map, and hash_multimap. Below is an example of how you can use vector in the same way you would use an ordinary array of C. The vector takes the chore away of managing a complex allocation by hand.

```
vector<int> vec(3);
v[0]=2;
v[1]=v[0]+1;
v[2]=v[0]+v[1];
```

The STL, or std library of algorithms is a set of generic routines that can be used across many types. One such type is collections which provide data structures for holding objects in variable ranges (think maps and sets). There's one particular algorithm called "reverse". It takes two arguments: an element range [Begin], and all elements greater than or equal to this first value. Reverse will do nothing unless these conditions hold true.

```
double arr[6] = {7.6,2.3,2.7,7.2,5.1,9.8};
reverse(arr, arr+6);
for(int i=0;i<6;++i)
        cout << "arr[" << i << "] = " <<
arr[i];
```

7.3 How Difficult Is It to Learn Programming?

Programming is usually perceived as being very difficult to learn and comprehend by the majority of non-technical people and as being reserved for super brains or geeks. However, although programming may indeed be a challenging skill to master, it is not a particularly demanding activity that requires months or years of study to master. While it is true that practice makes perfect, and the additional months and years may enable you to develop your programming abilities and become a better programmer, getting started is not difficult, and anybody with an internet connection and a computer can learn to program.

Many programming classes in school would have you begin by studying Visual Basic or C#, or any other language that is reasonably straightforward to learn and easy to comprehend, and then go from there. However, programming experts suggest that students or those interested in learning should begin with a high-level language such as C ++ or Java to grasp the ideas of Object-Oriented Programming, often known as OOP, and get familiar with the notions of classes, methods, and objects. It is preferable to learn from technical books since they are often fairly extensive and provide a variety of tasks to do, as well as examples and snippets of code to examine. They are, on the other hand, often fairly costly, with costs ranging from twenty dollars to more than sixty dollars. This may dissuade a significant number of individuals from participating and compel them to learn via the Internet. While this is not a negative technique in and of itself, you will not receive the same learning experience from it that you would get from a technical book from your local bookstore or library, for example.

Chapter 8

"Hello World!" application in C ++

The "Hello-World!" application is the very first program that a newbie should learn; in computer science, it is almost considered a tradition, to begin with, the Hello World program. If you wish to develop a program in C ++, you must follow a set of rules that must be followed. This collection of rules is referred to as syntax, and you will be able to grasp it in conjunction with the Hello World program.

```
1   #include<iostream>
2   using namespace std;
3
4   int main()
5   {
6
7       cout<<"Hello World!"<<endl;
8       return 0;
9
10  }
```

#includes<iostream> is a header file that is responsible for introducing features to the application. It is found in line 1. It is these preset functions that give you the functionality you want when building a program that is included inside these header files. The iostream header file provides definitions for cin, cout, and other functions that assist you in taking input from the user and displaying the results. To add a header file into a program the preprocessor #include is used while it is being built. The use of STD as a standard namespace indicates that you are utilizing the object and variable names from the standard library in line 2, which is an advantage over using other namespaces. The INT main () function, often known as the main function, is defined in line 3 and is an important aspect of each program. For example:

```
#include <iostream>
int main() {
        std::cout << "Welcome to world of
programming.";
        return 0;
}
```

Outcome:

```
Welcome to world of programming.
```

The first function is always the main function and is called when a program is executed. Cout is an object at line 7 that is used to print the output of the program when it is executed. For example, with this line, you will print the message Hello, World! In line 8, the return value of 0 indicates that nothing will be returned in this program. In this C ++ fundamentals course, you will get an understanding of data types and variables. If you recall from Lesson 1, "Getting Started," your very first C ++ program did nothing more than print a basic "Hello, World" line on the computer screen. Although this program comprises some of the most crucial and fundamental building elements, it is not a complete program.

8.1 Components of C ++ Program

This C ++ program is separated into two sections: the preprocessor directives beginning with a # and the main body of the program beginning with the INT main directive (). A preprocessor, as the name implies, is a tool that runs before the actual compilation process occurs. Preprocessor directives are instructions delivered to the preprocessor and are already followed by the pound symbol # The directive #include filename> informs the preprocessor to take the contents of the file (in this case, the iostream) and include it at the line in which the directive is written.

In Line 8, the iostream header file is standard to enables the use of STD::cout, which is enabled by the presence of the iostream header file, to display "Hello World." In other words, the compiler was able to generate Line 8 because we instructed the preprocessor to use the definition of STD::cout in the include statement. This is the program's main body, as specified by the function main, which comes after the preprocessing instructions (). The execution of a C ++ program always begins at this point. It is common practice to declare the function main() with an INT before it in the definition. The method main () returns an int, which is an acronym for integer. Talk about Line 8, which is the one that truly achieves the program's main purpose! The phrase cout (also known as "console-out" or "see-out") writes the message "Hello World" to the display console, commonly known as the screen.

You're inserting the string "Hello World" into the cout stream, which is defined in the standard STD namespace (thus, STD::cout), and you're doing it on this line by using the operator for inserting streams. The default end-of-line (STD::endl) character is used to end a line, and entering it into a stream is equivalent to inserting a carriage return (cr). It should be noted that the stream insertion operator () is used whenever a new entity must be added to the stream of entities. The benefit of utilizing streams in C ++ is that various stream types have equivalent stream semantics, enabling you to perform different operations on the same text and get different outputs.

Inserting into a file instead of a console, for example, would use the same insertion operator on a STD::fstream instead of a STD::cout to get the same result. As time passes, dealing with streams gets more natural, and if you become used to working with one stream (such as cout, which transmits text to the console), you'll find it easy to work with others (such as stream, which helps save files to the disk). Unless otherwise stated, C ++ functions must return a value unless otherwise specified. Furthermore, the procedure main () always returns an integer. When an application quits on its own, the operating system receives an integer value (OS). Depending on the nature of your program, this integer number might be highly significant, as most operating systems enable you to query the return result of a regularly terminated application. In many cases, one program launches another, and the parent application (which launched the child application) wants to know whether or not the child application (which was started) completed its function properly. The return value of main () can be used to inform the parent application if the action was successful or not.

Because the artefact (cout) that you want to call is located in the standard (STD) namespace, which you used in the application, you used STD:cout rather than just cout:

```
#include <iostream>
main()
{
    std::cout << "Welcome to world of
Programming";
    return 0;
}
```

So, what are namespaces and how do they function? Assume you didn't use the namespace qualifier while using cout, and that cout was available in two places known to the compiler. In this scenario, which one should the compiler choose to run cout? As a result, there is a conflict and, as predicted, the compilation fails.

This is where the use of namespaces may help. Namespaces are names assigned to parts of code to limit the possibility of a naming conflict happening. By using the std::cout command line parameter, you may direct the compiler to use the only cout available in the STD namespace. To invoke functions, the namespace STD (pronounced "standard") is utilized. When utilizing cout and other related features that are located in the same namespace as cout, many programmers find it inconvenient to have to add the STD namespace specifier to their code over and over again.

8.2 C ++ Library Files

The C ++ Standard Library is divided into two components, which are described below.

The Standard Function Library is a collection The Standardized Function Library is a collection of generic, independent functions which are unrelated to either particular class or type. The C programming language's function-library serves as the foundation for the function-library.

The "Object-Oriented Class Library" (OCL) is a repository of classes and associated methods. Below is a list of a few various different types. The Standard C ++ Library comprises all of the

Standardized C libraries with extensions and adjustments to ensure type-safety. Below is a list of a few various different types:

\<cstdlib\> – General purpose utilities like program control, dynamic memory allocation, random numbers, sort and search

\<csignal\> –Functions and macro constants for signal management(SIGINT, etc.)

\<csetjmp\> –Macro (and function) that saves (and jumps) to an execution context

\<cstdarg\> – Handling of variable length argument lists

\<typeinfo\> – Runtime type information utilities

\<bitset\> – class template of std::bitset

\<functional\> – Function objects, Function invocations, Bind operations and Reference wrappers

\<utility\> – Various utility components

\<ctime\> – C-style time/date utilites

\<cstddef\> – standard macros and typedefs

\<typeindex\> – Wrapper around type_info object, can be used as index in unordered associative containers as well as ordered

\<type_traits\> – Compile-time type information

\<chrono\> – C ++ time utilities

\<initializer_list\> –Library that defines a lightweight proxy object and provides access to a plethora of objects: const T.

Chapter 9

Data Types & Variables in C ++

Take a step back and learn about the components of a computer and how it operates before diving into the usage and use of variables in a programming language. All computers, smartphones, and other programmable devices are equipped with a microprocessor and a limited quantity of RAM (random access memory) for temporary storage (RAM). In addition, many technologies enable data to be saved on a storage device, such as a hard drive, for later retrieval and analysis. The microprocessor is responsible for executing your application, and to do so, it communicates with the RAM to retrieve the binary code to be executed, as well as the data associated with it, which includes the information displayed on the screen and the information entered by the user, to be executed. The RAM itself may be thought of as a storage facility, similar to a row of lockers in a hostel, with each locker being assigned a number or an address. To access a specific address in memory, such as location 578, the processor must be instructed to either read a value from or write a value to that position through an instruction. The examples that follow will assist you in understanding what variables are and how to use them.

Consider the following scenario: you are building software that will multiply two integers given by the user. Each multiplicand and multiplier is sent into your software sequentially by the user, and you must store each of them so that they may be used to multiply later on in the program. Based on what you intend to do with the result of the multiplication, you may wish to save the result of the multiplication for later use in your application. To store the numbers, you would need to explicitly specify memory addresses (such as 578), which would be time-consuming and error-prone because you would have to worry about either accidentally overwriting existing data at the location of your data being overwritten in the future. The compiler gets informed by the variable type attribute concerning the sort of data that the variable may contain, and the compiler allocates the appropriate amount of space for it. The programmer's choice of name acts as a friendlier substitute for the memory address where the variable's value is stored.

You cannot be certain of the contents of a memory region till the initial value is set, which may be detrimental to the program's performance. As a result, initialization is not required. However, it is often recommended as a good programming practice. Using variables in a program that multiplies two integers entered by the user Ordinary variables, like the ones we've declared so far, have a well-defined scope within which they are valid and may be used to perform their functions. When variables are used outside of their scope, the names of the variables will not be recognized by the compiler, and your program will not be able to run. A variable is an unnamed item that the compiler is unaware of when it is used outside of its scope.

9.1 Variable Declaration in C ++

Additionally, C ++ supports the definition of many additional variables, which we will explore in more detail in the following chapters, such as Calculation, Identifier (including frames), Reference (including references to other variables), Data structures, and classes. A variable statement instructs the compiler what further storage the variable will receive throughout the merging process. A variable statement provides the sort of data it contains and contains a set of one or maybe more variables, each with its own definition. Here, The type has to be a valid C++ data type, such as float, double, int, char, char, or bool, or any other specified by the user., among other things, and the dynamic list may contain one or more comma-separated identifiers, and the first reference name is first in the list. When you see the line int.i.i.j.k., you know that you are both announcing and explaining the INT variable. It also tells the producer to build three INT variables of the same name: inti, intj, and into.

During the declaration process, a variable can be activated (i.e., given the initial value). The launcher is represented by an equal sign. The following variable default values have a fixed storage duration when no launcher is specified: the static duration variables are automatically started NULL (all bytes have a value of 0); the default values for all other variables are unknown. The dynamic declaration gives the compiler the confidence that there is only one variation of the specified type and name, allowing the compiler to proceed with the entire compilation without knowing all the details about the variation. Contrary to the fact that a flexible announcement is only relevant during integration, the producer needs a real definition of variation during system integration. When many files are used, and the variables are created inside one of the files that will be accessible during the application connection, a flexible announcement may be quite beneficial. At any point in the system, one will utilize a foreign term to describe a variable. While the variable may be declared multiple times within a C++ program, it can only be specified once within a file, task, or code block.no matter how many times it is announced. The syntax is as follows:

```
Datatype   variable_name;
int   a;
```

9.2 Types of Data in C ++

During the definition of all variables, the data type keyword is used to restrict the type of data that could be saved. We can define data types as forms of information utilized to store various types of data. Composer provides variable memory whenever defined in C ++, and the amount of memory provided depends on the type of data being declared variable. Depending on the data format, different amounts of RAM are required. Classic data types are types of built-in or pre-set that can be used by the user directly to create variations. Classical data types are pre-determined data types that can be used by the user directly to declare alternatives—for example, int, char, float, bool, and so on. Types of Data Received: Types of Data Received are types of data based on old or built-in

94

data types and are used to store information about objects. Types of Data Specified or Specified by User: These are the types of data defined by the user himself. For example, in C ++, you could define a class or structure.

- Total number: The keyword INT is used to refer to all types of data. When working with integers, the standard requirement is 4 bytes of memory space, the range is - 2147483648 to 2147483647.

- Character: A character type is used to store characters in a text file. The keyword char is used to describe the type of character data. The letters usually take up a single memory space and can be found in the range from -128 to 127 or 0 to 255, respectively. For example:

The Syntax: char [variable name]=value;

```
E.g: ch1{ ' a ' };
```

- On a computer, a type of Boolean data is used to store sensible or rational values, such as true or false. The Boolean variable can store true or false values. The keyword bool is used to describe a type of Boolean data. Here's an example utilizing perl.

```
use strict;
my($Username, $Userpassword);
print "\nWrite UserName: ";
chomp($Username = <STDIN>);
print "\nEnter Password: ";
chomp($Userpassword = <STDIN>);
```

```
if (($Username eq "Jhon") && ($password eq
"12345")) {
     print "Loggedin\n";
}
else {
     print "Fail to loggin\n";
     die;
}
```

- Maintain accurate floating-point numbers (or decimal values) using the Floating Point data type. The float keyword is used to describe the type of floating-point data. The memory space for the floating-point variables is usually the size of 4 bytes.

- Double accurate floating point or decimal value is maintained using Double Floating Point data, also known as double accurate floating point or double decimal value. Double the keyword used to describe a type of double-float point data. Dual variables take an average of 8 bytes of memory for activation.

- Vanity: The word "vanity" refers to anything that has no value. Valuable data type describes a non-value business. In the case of non-refundable operations, a Void data type is used.

- Wide Character: The uppercase data type is the same as the uppercase data type, but has a larger size than the standard 8-bit data type. Comprehensive Character Data (w-Char-T) is used to represent this type of data. It is usually 2 or 4 bytes.

96

Chapter 10

Operators in C ++

A programming language's Operators seem to be the fundamental building elements of every computer language. Operators may be thought of as symbols that assist us in doing certain mathematical and logical operations on operands, as opposed to variables. On the other hand, we could claim that an operator is in charge of the operands' operation. For example, the operator '+' is used to indicate addition. There are two operands in this equation: 'a' and 'b'. The addition operator is represented by the symbol +. The (+ operator) instructs the compiler for combining the values of the 'a' and 'b', which are operands.

Without the employment of operators, the capabilities of the C/C ++ programming language would be significantly reduced. C/C ++ includes a large number of built-in operators, which may be divided into six types: Algebraic and Numerical Operators Relational Operators are used to establish relationships between two or more entities. Logical Operators are a kind of logic that may be used to solve problems. Bitwise operators are a kind of operator that operates on bits. Assignment Operators are a kind of assignment operator. Other company's operator's further investigation has been conducted into the following operators: On these operators, operands are employed to perform both arithmetic and mathematical operations. which are referred to as arithmetic/mathematical operators. Examples are (+, -, *, /, percent, ++, and –).

10.1 There are two kinds of arithmetic operators

Monotonic Operators: Monotonic operators are those that work with a single operand and a pair of operands. For example, the Increment (++) and Decrement (–) operators are both used in programming. Operation with Two Opponents: those operators which are binary are used to operate on or work with two operands. Let's take an example the operations Addition (+), Subtraction (-), Multiplication (*), and Division (/) are all possible combinations. In a mathematical equation, relational-operators are intended to compare the values of two operands. For instance, determining If an operand is identical towards the other operand's value or not, or if the first operand is larger than the other one or not, and so on. Some operators are (==, >=, =), and others are not. (For further information, see this chapter.) The Bitwise operators are used to perform certain operations on the operands at the bit level. Firstly, the operators are transformed to bit-level representations, and then the calculations on operand are done.

Expressions like (+), (-), (*), and other similar operations may be done at the bit-level for quicker computation. A bitwise AND operator, represented as the & operator in programming languages such as Java, accepts two integers as operands and applies the AND operator to all of the bits in both numbers. In the case of an AND, the outcome is 1 only if both bits are 1. When assigning a value to a variable, assignment operators are utilized to do so. Assigning values to variables is accomplished using the assignment operator, which takes a variable as its left side operand and a value as its right side operand.

Unless otherwise specified, the right-side value must be similar to the data type on the left-side variable; otherwise, the compiler will raise an issue/error. Here are examples of several types of assessment operators: a. "=": "=" is the most straightforward assessment operator. This operator takes the value on the right-hand-side as an input and assigns it to the variable on the left-hand-side. Here, "+=" is a concatenation of the operator "plus" and "equals." The operator takes the value of the variable on left-side towards the value of the variable on the right-side before assigning the outcome to the variable on the left-side., as shown in the example below.

It is made up of the operators "-=" and "=," and it is used to denote the absence of a prefix. That operator - the value of the variable on the left-side from the number here on the right-side, before assigning the outcome towards the variable on the left-side. As seen in the example below. "*=": here operator is the combo of the '*' as-well-as the '=' operators, and it is used to denote a condition. After multiplying the left variable's value by the right variable's value, this operator returns the answer in the direction of the leftmost variable, which is a one-to-one correspondence.

Chapter 11

Loops & Functions in C ++

To this point, you've seen how to have your program respond differently depending on whether variables contain various values. What happens if he wishes to conduct another addition or multiplication operation, or perhaps five more in a row? When you need to repeat the execution of previously written code, you're at the right place. This is the point at which you must write a loop.

The Loop statement need only be typed at first before the loop will get executed ten times, as shown in the example. In programming, a loop is a set of commands which gets repeated till a specified target is met. Following the completion of an operation, such as receiving and modifying data, a condition, such as assessing if a counter has reached the required number, is confirmed. If the count does not reach the specified numbers and the following instructions in this process and instruction returns to the first and repeats its. If the counter doesn't reach the specified number, the following instructions in the series return to the very first instruction redo it. If the target is fulfilled, the afterward successive instruction which is eventually falling through or branches outside of the loop, and the loop is ended. Loops are classified into two types: inner and outward. The ECLs (Entry-Controlled-Loops). In this type of loop, the trial condition is checked prior to attending the loop body. The loop body is then tested once the test condition is passed. Loops with entrance-controlled entry are the for Loop and the While Loop. In this form of a loop, the test condition is checked or assessed on the end-side of this loop body, referred to as an "exit controlled loop". The body of the loop will thus be executed at least once, regardless of whether the test condition is true or false in the conditional statement.

Exit-controlled loops are represented by the do-while loop. It is possible to build a (for loop), which is a control structure of repetition, that will be run a particular time number. The loop enables us to do a lot of operations in a single line by grouping them. The for loop is controlled by a loop variable, which is defined as follows: Then verify whether the value of this loop variable is less than or more than the value of the counter variable. If factual, the loop's body will run, and the loop variable is updated appropriately. These steps will be followed until the departure condition is met. Expression of Initialization (in English): It is necessary to initialization the center of the loop counter to a certain value in this phrase. As an illustration: INT i=1; the following is an example of a test-expression: Here, we must put the condition to the test. The loop's body will get executed, and we'll go on to the update expression if the condition illustrates true; on the other hand, we'll leave the for-loop and return. For instance: (i = 10; i = 10; i = 10;) update the expression. After the loop, the body has been executed, and expression increases or decreases the value of the loop variable by a specified amount. For example: i++;

11.1 While Loop

The iterations are known ahead of time. This means that we know how many runs the body of the loop needs in order to get executed. This was discovered when researching for the loop. And these loops are utilized in cases when we don't know the precise number of iterations of a loop we will be performing in advance. The execution of the loop is ended according to the outcome of the condition of the test. Already said, a loop is composed mostly of these statements, and expressions are initialization, test, and update expressions. The syntax of these loops is (for, while, and do-while) changes only in the order in which these 3 statements are.

Initialization expression;

```
While (test-expression)
{
    // /statements

    Update-expression ;}
```

11.2 Do while loop

In this, the implementation of the loop is also halted based on the result of the test condition. Due to the fact that the condition is verified after the body of the loop, the "do-while loop" differs from the other two loops in that it is controlled by exiting it. The other two loops, on the other hand, are entrance controlled. In a "do-while loop", loop's body will be executed at least once regardless of the test circumstance. The evaluation of the test condition (i1) in the preceding software results in a misleading result. However, the structure of the loop executes only one time. Check out how to print numbers 1 through 5:

```cpp
#include <iostream>

using namespace std;

int main() {
        int loopcounter = 1;

        // while loop from 1 to 5
        while (loopcounter <= 5) {
                cout << loopcounter << " ";
                ++loopcounter;
        }
        return 0;
}
```

Outcome:

```
12345
```

11.3 What about an Infinite Loop?

An endless loop is called an "infinite loop" and is a part of code that does not have a functioning exit, causing it to continue endlessly without stopping. An endless loop happens when the evaluation of the condition will be true on an unlimited number of occasions. Normally, this indicates a clerical mistake. When we know the iteration number ahead of time, i.e. when the loop body is required to be run is identified, the loop body is used. Where the number of iterations performed is unidentified, but the condition of loop termination is identified. If the code has to be performed, like in menu-driven systems, then a do-while loop should be used.

For instance:

```
#include <iostream>
int main() {
        while (1 == 1) {
                std::cout << "I love CPP" <<
endl;
        }
}
```

Outcome:

```
I love CPP
I love CPP
I love CPP
I love CPP
```

11.4 For loop

Because it enables for an initialization statement to be run just once (usually to establish a counter), checking for an exit condition (often using this counter), and executing an action after every loop, the statement is more advanced than the while statement (typically incrementing or modifying this counter). An example of this is the for loop, which allows you to construct a counter variable with an initial value, compare the current values against a set of exit conditions at the beginning of each loop, and alter the value of the counter variable after each loop. During this session, you learned how to design conditional statements that establish alternate execution routes and cause code blocks to repeat in a loop, among other things. You learned how to use the if-else construct and switch-case statements to handle distinct circumstances if variables have different values. When learning about loops, you were taught about the go-to command, but you were also advised against using it since it has the potential to produce code that is difficult to comprehend. You learned how to write loops in C ++ by using the while, do...while, and for statements. You learned how to make the loops repeat indefinitely to build infinite loops, as well as how to manage them more effectively using the continue and break commands. For instance:

```
int count = 1;
do {
        // code in loop
} while (count == 1);
```

The preceding program demonstrates that this condition is accurate will run infinitely.

11.5 Functions in C ++

Up to this point in the book, you've encountered basic programs in which all of the programming work is contained in the main function (). This is particularly useful for really little programs and apps. The contents of main () will inevitably grow in size and complexity as your program grows in size and complexity unless you choose to organize your program via the use of functions. Functions provide a mechanism to compartmentalize and organize the logic that governs the execution of your program. They provide you with the ability to divide the contents of your application into logical chunks that are called one after another in a sequential manner.

As a result, a function is a subprogram that may accept arguments and return a value, and it must be called to complete its work. In this session, you will understand why it is necessary to program functions.

```
To declare a function, you can use this
syntax:
returnType NameOfFuntion(param1, param2) {
     // Body of funtion
}
example of function declaration :
void greet() {
     cout << "I love CPP";
}
```

Unless the function is specified with a void which is the return type, a return statement must be included in the code. Because the function has been defined as one that returns a double, Area () is required to return a value in this circumstance. The statement block comprises statements enclosed in open and closed braces (...), which are executed when the function is invoked. The statement block is divided into two parts. Area () computes the area of a circle by using the input parameter radius, which includes the radius as an argument supplied by the caller, and the radius as an argument sent by the caller. Using the [greet( )] function requires the need to call it.

For example:

```
int main() {

    // calling a function
    greet();

}
```

You can create two functions consisting an identical name and return value but with distinct debates in each. To enable you to modify more data or arguments in a function call, you may construct a function such that its parameters do not need to be generated and destroyed inside the function call; instead, you can utilize references that remain valid even after the function has departed. Arrays are sent to functions in this part, as is function overloading, and providing parameters by reference to functions are covered throughout this section. Overloaded functions contain an identical name and return type as the original function but hold a distinctive set of arguments or a distinctive set of parameters than the original function. Extending the functionality of a function by providing more than one form of output may be very beneficial in situations where a function with a certain name that generates a specific type of output has to be run with multiple sets of inputs. Consider the following scenario: you are responsible for building an application that computes the circumference of a circle and the circumference of a cylinder. The radius of a circle is a parameter in the function that computes the circumference of a circle. In addition to the cylinder's radius, the other function that computes the area of the cylinder requires the height of the cylinder.

Both functions must return data of the same type, including the area, to be successful. As a result, C ++ allows you to construct two overloaded functions, both named Area, both returning double, but one that just accepts the radius as input and another that accepts both the height and the radius as input. Although it is not necessary to understand how a function call is implemented at the microprocessor level, you may find it fascinating to learn more about it. In understanding this, it becomes easier to see why C ++ provides you with the option of writing inline functions, which will be discussed more in this section. Instruction about the called function at an inconsequential memory address is executed by the microprocessor when the function is called, which is basically what a function call is all about. After it has finished executing the instructions contained inside the function, it returns to the point where it was before. To put this reasoning into action, the compiler turns your function call into a CALL instruction that can be executed by the CPU. A function is a group of instructions that accepts inputs and conducts a specific activity, and returns the end.

The goal is to group tasks that are performed often or regularly and turn them into functions so that we may call the function instead of writing the same code over and again for various inputs. Functions assist us in decreasing the amount of redundant code in our programs. If a function must be performed in various locations across software, rather than writing the same code again and over, we may design a function that can be called from anywhere. This also helps with maintenance since we just have to make one modification if we want to make changes to the functionality in the future. Code becomes more modular as a result of the use of functions. Let's say you have a large file with numerous lines of code. When you break down a large piece of code into smaller pieces, it becomes much easier to comprehend and utilize. Functions are used to abstract information. For example, we may utilize library functions without having to worry about how they are implemented inside. Using a function declaration, the compiler can find out how many arguments the function accepts, what data types the parameters are, and what sort of return the function will produce.

The inclusion of parameter names in the function declaration is optional; however, it is required to include them in the definition of the function. The next section is an example of the declaration of a function. (The names of the parameters are not included in the following declarations.) Pass by Value: This is how you pass by value. Parameters or arguments, can be utilized to identify a function. Which passed when declaring the function.

Consider the following illustration:

```
void DisplayNumber(int n) {
        cout << n;
}
```

Preceding, The int[n] is the parameter of function.

The CPU continues to analyze them until it reaches the RET statement (which is the microprocessor's return code that you defined). The RET statement causes the microprocessor to pop the address specified in the CALL instruction from the stack that was previously saved. There is a pointer here that points to a spot in the calling function where the execution should proceed. As a result, the microprocessor is returned to the caller and the process resumes where it left off. As a consequence, a conventional function call is converted into a CALL instruction, which results in stack operations and a microprocessor execution shift to the function, among other things. For the most part, this is a rapid process that takes place beneath the hood. What if, on the other hand, your role is a relatively basic one, such as the following? "Using Variables, Declaring Constants" was the third lesson in which you learned about the term auto. It allows you to defer the determination of variable type to the compiler, which does base on the initialization value supplied to the variable in question.

Starting with C ++14, The same holds accurate for both functions and variables. Instead of declaring the return type, you would use auto, which would allow the compiler to guess the return type for you based on the return values that you program. With the introduction of C ++11, lambda functions have become more useful in the use of STL algorithms to sort and process data. Typically, a sort function needs you to provide a binary criterion to work. This is a function that compares two inputs and returns true if one of them is smaller than the other, otherwise false, and so assisting in the determination of the order of items in a sorting process. Predicates of this kind are often implemented as operators in a class, resulting in a time-consuming chunk of code. In this session, you learned the fundamentals of modular programming from the ground up.

You learned how functions might assist you in better structuring your code as well as in reusing algorithms that you have written. This lesson covered the concepts of function parameters and return values, parameter defaults that the caller may modify, and parameters including arguments given by reference. You learned how to pass arrays, and you also learned how to write overloaded functions that contain an identical name and return type yet a unique set of parameters. Last but not least, you got a sneak peek at what lambda functions are and how they work. Lambda functions, which are completely new as of C ++, have the potential to fundamentally alter the way C ++ programs are built in the future, particularly when employing the STL. The program's execution does not conclude.

There are while(true) and for (;;) loops that do the same thing, so it is not necessarily bad; but, a recursive function call uses more and more stack space, which is limited and ultimately runs out, resulting in an application crash due to a stack overflow. That depends on the situation. While inlining every function saves space, it also causes code bloat by causing functions that are used in several locations. However, aside from that, most current compilers are better judges of which calls may be inlined and conduct this task on the programmer's behalf, depending on the compiler's performance options. For function overloading to work, two functions with the same name must have the same return types, or else they will fail. The name has been used twice in what your compiler expects to be two functions with separate names in this situation, and your compiler displays an error as a result.

Chapter 12

Object-Oriented
Programming using C ++

The main driving force for the development of the object-oriented method was the need to correct some of the problems that had been discovered in the procedural technique. The development of Software development is still a dynamic process. Fresh apparatuses and procedures are introduced one after another in rapid succession. To keep up with the rising complexity of software products and the industry's high level of competition and software industry and software engineers must constantly seek out innovative approaches to software development and design. This is becoming increasingly important given the growing complication of software systems and the industry's highly competitive character for years, engineers have experimented with a wide range of tools, methodologies, and processes to better manage the so that super quality software may be produced with the enhanced efficiency and those software development process should be optimized. A significant amount of the conceptual underpinning for the object-oriented paradigm is drawn from general systems theory. A system may be thought of as a collection of elements that interact with one another to achieve certain goals. Both tangible items, such as equipment and people, as well as abstract notions like data files and operations, may be represented by entities. Entities, also known as objects in object-oriented analysis, are the building blocks of the analysis. The term implies the object-oriented paradigm focuses more emphasis on goods that serve to encapsulate data and methods than the traditional paradigm. Because they play a major part in all the phases of the development of software, there is an overlap of the high degree of repetition across the various phases.

In nature, the whole development process is transformed into an evolutionary process. As a result, a Graphical representation of the object-oriented version of the SDLC must include the two features of overlap and iteration. As a result of this choice, a "fountain model" replaces the existing "waterfall model." It is the methods of specifying software Object-oriented analysis that refers to the requirement in terms of actual objects, their behavior, and their relationships. Object-oriented design, nevertheless, in contrast, converts requirements of software into object specification and generates hierarchies of the class by which objects may be produced. OOP mentions the usage of objects in this language, like C ++, to accomplish the desired outcome. With OOA, we have a simple but very powerful system for recognizing objects, which serves as the building blocks of the program that will be produced. It is primarily concerned about the deconstruction of difficulty into its elements' components and the establishment of a model for explanations of the operations of a computer system. The mappings of items in the issue into objects in the solution space, well as the creation of a general structure and computational representations of the system, are the primary concerns of the OOD. When designing the class member functions that offer services, this step often uses the method of (bottom-up) to construct the structure of the system and the top-down functional decomposition technique to construct the system's structure. Constructing hierarchical hierarchies, identifying abstract classes, and simplifying the communication between objects inside a system are all critical tasks. Some of the issues for the design stage include the reusability of classes from earlier designs, the grouping of objects into subsystems, and the creation of acceptable protocols. Knowing that a class includes both data and code is important if you have created programs using C ++ Builder. You also know that classes may be manipulated both during the design process and during the runtime. In that sense, you've progressed to the level of component user. It is necessary to deal with classes in ways that application developers would never have to deal with when creating new components. In addition, you attempt to keep the inner workings of the component hidden from the developers who will be using it. You may construct adaptable, reusable components by selecting suitable ancestors for your components, developing interfaces that expose just the attributes and methods that developers want, and following the other suggestions in the following areas. The following subjects, which are related to object-oriented programming (OOP), should be acquainted with you before you begin constructing components. Creating new classifications in contrast to application developers, component writers generate new classes, and application developers change the instances of classes created by the component writers. A type is roughly the same as a class. In your job as a programmer, you are always dealing with types and instances, even if you do not refer to them as such. If you want to construct variables of a certain type, such as int, you may do so. Generally speaking, classes are more sophisticated than basic data types, yet they function in the same way: By giving various values to instances of the same type, you may conduct a variety of operations on those instances.

12.1 Tips for Real Object-oriented Programming in C ++

According to the Law of Spurgeon, ninety percent of anything is garbage. This is absolutely in the field of software development, this is especially true, and it is particularly true in the case of object-oriented programming, as well as other programming languages. This is mostly due to the widespread usage and difficulty of C ++; it is the most widely used object-oriented programming language, although only a small percentage of the population is proficient in its use. When you combine this with the reality that only a small percentage of programmers understand the object-oriented programming paradigm, sloppy code has a certain prescription. Volumes may be written and have published on the subject of how to construct good object-oriented design using the C ++ programming language.

Make progress on the first design of the class before deciding on the specific order in which operations should be performed. Even though many programmers consider themselves to be practicing object-oriented programming, they have used some external object-oriented trappings with structured programming. In an ideal situation, one would first choose a group of software objects that serve as a logical abstraction of the program. After that, focus on the order of operations. It should be noted that this is by no means a hard and fast rule since the process of constructing this sequence often exposes cases in which the design of the object might be improved. Design patterns come to mind while thinking about this. When someone uses design patterns, they may rely on years of basic problem-solving knowledge gained within the community of computer science. Instead of creating the wheel, why not simply use one that is already in existence? Whenever feasible, use 'const' objects and 'const' functions to ensure that your code is consistent. Declare an object to be a 'const' object if you are certain that the data contained inside the object will never be updated. This will prevent you, or even worse, a naive coworker, from mistakenly altering the state of the object in the future. Of course, to effectively enforce this requirement, one needs additionally declare the necessary member functions will be constant as well. It is best not to use the public 'get' and 'set' member methods.

Getter and setter aren't intrinsically harmful; nonetheless, they are frequently a symptom of poor software abstraction when they are used. These functions implicitly compel in the term of internal data of object user thoughts (that is, whatever it is that functions are retrieving or setting), and such information should be kept concealed from the object's user, as far as is reasonably possible. Getter and setter have their place, but please utilize them only when necessary. Avoid the use of double indirection. Given that C programmers have no choice but to deal with pointers, they have become used to the practice of using pointers in their code to refer to other points in the code. As a result of the familiar difficulties of NULL references and pointer arithmetic, this may often result in ambiguous or even incomprehensible code. C ++ programmers, on the other hand, are not restricted in this manner, owing to C ++'s built-in support for variable references; that is, instead of using variable references, one can always use references to pointers which significantly simplifies the understanding and maintenance of the code. A hint: If a C ++ programmer uses double indirection, it's a good bet he's still thinking like a beginner C programmer!

12.2 Concepts of Object-Oriented Programming in C ++

A very recent development in the history of programming languages is the appearance of the programming style that we often refer to as object-oriented programming (OOP). This is a unique and very handy design that may be used in a variety of scenarios. Structured programming, which relies primarily on extensive usage of procedures, functions, and pointers, as well as other advance or less developed data types, was intended to address the limitations of this approach.

Structured programming is beneficial even for modest software systems or non-graphic applications. It should be avoided when working with big programs that have visual aspects, for which object-oriented programming is highly recommended instead. To be object-oriented is to organize software resources in the form of a Both data structures and the processing actions that they execute are

117

included in this collection of separate and discrete items. Object-oriented in programming, which is an extension of structured programming, data structures, and processing activities are only loosely connected. Each object has its own identity and is unique from the others. An object is defined as an abstract idea with certain specific and helpful elements for applications that are designed to be useful and specific.

Objects have two distinct purposes. They aid in the comprehension of the issue to be addressed, and - they serve as a foundation for the execution of the solution. A class of objects is a collection of objects with comparable features that are all contained inside a single container. Similarity exists in both the descriptions (data and characteristics) and the behavior of the two systems (functions or methods). Attributes are characteristics that distinguish one object type from another. Each property is assigned a specific value, which may be changed at any time throughout the life cycle of objects. If two or more items are all in the same collection, they may have the same or distinct values for the same attribute. Operations and methods are processing functions that are applied to objects belonging to a certain class of objects. Objects belonging to the same class have access to the unique set of methods which in turn may accept any number of extra inputs. It is necessary to build an object to be able to apply numerous methods to it (defined).

The process of object definition is referred to as instantiation. When an item has completed its purpose, it is eliminated from the scene. Abstraction is a basic human quality that enables us to construct models and, as a result, deal with complexity and ambiguity. In every sphere of human endeavor, the project method is based on the development of a model that will aid in the understanding of the issue to be solved. The field of software engineering is no exception. The vital core parts are separated from the non-essential ones via the process of abstraction. As a result, there may be numerous appropriate models for each issue. Structured programming has made significant strides ahead in the software engineering business, outlining three viewpoints that must be considered to correctly handle any application.

The dynamic and static models, and also functional models, are the three views, sometimes known as models, from which to see the world. In today's world, there are a variety of object-oriented approaches that are employed in the analyzing, designing, and implementing of software resources. The OMT (Object Modeling Technique) technique is one of the methodologies in modeling that may be used. In this type of modeling, the many growth phases are planned, and items and their connections are represented graphically to show how they relate to one another.

Chapter 13

Data Structure Using C ++

A s we all know, the C ++ programming language provides its users with a plethora of intriguing and helpful features and functions, and this is no exception. Furthermore, it provides support for object-oriented programming. In addition to performing certain big techniques like encapsulation, abstraction, inheritance, and polymorphism, you can also conduct some minor methods such as encoding and decoding. Data structures are a necessary and unavoidable component of programming in C ++ because of their use and need. We may execute operations on data with the assistance of data structures, such as data representation, storage, organization, and many more actions on data. Data structures allow you to arrange data in a certain manner so that it may be utilized more efficiently in a variety of applications. There are a variety of methods for organizing the information in memory. It is important to understand that it is not a programming language but rather a collection of methods that may be used to organize data into memory in any programming language. The array data structure is used to hold a list of things in the example below. Arrays are essentially a collection of data kinds that are stored in contiguous memory regions that are identical to one another.

It is capable of storing basic sorts of data such as int, char, float, double, and so on. With the use of arrays, a programmer may quickly and simply retrieve the items in a collection. As an example, if you wish to record the marks of 20 students, you may try declaring 20 variables such as student1 marks, student2 marks, and so on. If I told you that all of this can be accomplished with only one variable, the answer would be "yes." You can get access to such components with the assistance of a few lines of code. A structure contains a collection of variables representing various types of data. All of which are known by the same name. Because both include collections of data of varying data kinds, they are comparable to classes in this regard.

You'd want to keep track of a person's identifying details, such as their names, nationality number, and yearly salary. To record this information individually, you may simply construct distinct variables for name, Citgo, and income. Creating a structure is accomplished through the use of the struct-statement, which creates a new type of data for the program.

Demonstration of the Formatting :

```
struct [structure tag] {
   member definition;
   member definition;
   ...
   member definition;
} [one or more structure variables];
```

13.1 Concepts of Data Structure in C ++

What is the best way to create better algorithms? This is one of the fundamental problems that every programmer wrestles with. Even software designers want more effective algorithms. The question is, how can we determine whether the algorithm is superior to the other? Isn't it sufficient that the job has been completed and the issue has been resolved? Not all of the time. Which of the following would you prefer: me solving the issue in 5 years or someone else coming up with a solution in 5 minutes? It is not a matter of having fast computers, but rather of having quick algorithms. The difficulty of an algorithm is used to determine the speed with which it executes. Generally speaking, an algorithm with logarithmic time complexity is regarded as superior to an algorithm with exponential time complexity, and so on.

With functions arguments, you'll be able to display certain information about things (book descriptions for example). Take a look a the sample below:

```
#include <iostream>
#include <cstring>

using namespace std;
struct Books {
      char   bookTitle[50];
      char   bookAuthor[50];
      char   bookSubject[100];
      int    bookId;
};
void showBook(struct Books book) {
```

```cpp
        cout << "Title of Book : " <<
book.bookTitle << "\n";
        cout << "Author of Book : " <<
book.bookAuthor << "\n";
        cout << "Subject of Book : " <<
book.bookSubject << "\n";
        cout << "Id of Book : " << book.bookId
<< "\n";
}

int main() {
        struct Books FisrtBook,SecondBook;

        strcpy(FisrtBook.bookTitle, "Cooking
Recipes");
        strcpy(FisrtBook.bookAuthor, "Sandy
Millan");
        strcpy(FisrtBook.bookSubject,
"Cooking");
        FisrtBook.bookId = 34563;

        strcpy(SecondBook.bookTitle,
"Mediterranean Cooking");
        strcpy(SecondBook.bookAuthor,
"Singh");
        strcpy(SecondBook.bookSubject,
"Cooking");
        SecondBook.bookId = 1224;

        showBook(FisrtBook);
        showBook(SecondBook);
        return 0;
}
```

After executing the preceding code, the end result would look like this:

```
First book title: Cooking Recipes
First book author: Sandy Millan
First book subject: Cooking
First book ID: 1224
Second book title: Mediterranean Cooking
Second book author: Singh
Second book subject: Cooking
Second book ID: 6400700
```

13.2 Linked Lists

Linked lists are a far more versatile means of storing and retrieving data than traditional databases. You are free to remove or add things anywhere on the page, and you may even dynamically add items without knowing how many items you will need in advance. The main drawback is that there is no way to get random access to the system. Stacks may be constructed using either arrays or linked lists, depending on the situation. They only allow for the insertion and removal of items from the LIFO order of precedence. The use of stacks is widespread, and they are used in many different applications, such as search algorithms and recursion. The structure of one node comes first.

The structure here:

```
struct Node {
  int data;
  struct Node *next;
};
```

It has two parts: The int data that holds value of the integer and the node, which represents a pointer called 'next'.

For a linked list, it's necessary to create a class that contains the necessary functions for controlling nodes:

```
#include<iostream>
int main() {

        class Node {
        public:
                int value;
                Node * pointertonextNode;
        };
}
```

13.3 Queue

A "queue" is a framework that operates on the first-in, first-out (FIFO) principle. Queues may be built using arrays or linked lists, as seen in the following example. Queues allow for the deletion of items from one end and the insertion of items from the other. There are many different forms of queues, such as circular queues: queues with two ends, queues with input restrictions, and so forth. Trees are used to arrange data hierarchically, making it easier to delete and add items to the database. We will look at the design of a simple example of a queue in C ++.

Here's one example that is easy to follow:

```
#include<queue>
#include<iostream>
using namespace std;
void Display(queue<int> q)
{
        queue <int> temp = q;
```

```
        while (!temp.empty())
        {
                cout<<"  "<<temp.front();
                temp.pop();
        }
        cout<<"\n";
}

int main()
{
        queue <int> m_queue;
        m_queue.push(89);
        m_queue.push(12);
        m_queue.push(23);
        cout << "Data in Queue: ";
        Display(m_queue);
        cout<<"Total Size:
"<<m_queue.size()<<"\n";
        cout<<"Front:
"<<m_queue.front()<<"\n";
        cout<<"Back: "<<m_queue.back()<<"\n";
        return 0;
}
```

The output:

```
Here is the Queue:  33 44 55
Size of Queue: 3
Front of Queue: 33
Back of Queue: 55
```

Chapter 14

Projects in C ++

You may complete a variety of tasks ranging from beginner to intermediate levels to put your C ++ skills to the test. During these tasks, you will learn something new, allowing you to get more acquainted with the most significant issues that will always be useful since you're working on real-time projects. You must first install an integrated development environment (IDE) before you can begin working on such projects. Visual Studio is available for download for free from the official website of Microsoft. Alternatively, you can download Code: Blocks directly from the developer's website.

To begin with, many students study their first programming languages are C and C ++, which is standard practice. They soon gain the ability to construct programs that include pointers, arrays, and function, as well as data structure and file handling, among other things. However, when it comes to creating a mini-game, an application, or a tiny project, combining all of these aspects into a single compact program becomes tough to do. The use of reference projects is usually beneficial in such situations. The C and C ++

projects available on our site will educate you on how we have started, provide you with ideas and themes for your projects, and help you to improve your programming abilities in C and C ++ as you go through the projects. You'll discover both short and basic crafts as well as lengthy and sophisticated ones on this page.

14.1 Why do developers create project ideas in C ++ rather than other programming languages?

There are many compelling reasons why those who work in the field of embedded systems and systems programming, which includes operating systems and hardware interfaces, seem to favor C ++ above any other programming language to learn for a variety of reasons. To begin, C ++, like C, is an open-source programming language, which makes it perfect for future adaptations and advancements. C ++ is comparable to C in that it is free to use and modify. In terms of technical abilities, it is a very simple coding language to learn, thanks to the fact that it is composed entirely of pure ideas and has a straightforward syntax.

The C ++ programming language, however, is a highly flexible and dynamic language that has enabled several technical accomplishments in sectors such as electrical devices, autos, robots, and a variety of others. This has been made feasible because developers have found it straightforward to incorporate C ++ into the operational frameworks of the many sectors in which they have worked. To summarize, not only is C ++ simple to script, but it is extremely compatible with a broad range of platforms and operating systems as well. As a consequence, C ++ may be used to create fresh technical inputs that were previously impossible. It is true that C ++, which is laden with the sweetness of C but with enhanced functionality, is the coding language of all future technologies.

14.2 Log-in and Registration System

This is among the simplest tasks to begin with when understanding the file-systems in C ++. This task incorporates a sign up process that requires users to provide their login details. A user folder containing the login details is generated following a successful enrollment. If no such user exists, an error message appears. When the user attempts to log in.

Follow this source code below to see how it's set up:

```
#include<iostream>
#include<fstream>
using namespace std;

struct EmailData
{
        char username[25];
        char password[25];
        void reg(int);
} obj[5];

void EmailData::reg(int id)
{
        cout<<"Enter Name:";
        cin >> username;
        cout << "Enter password:";
        cin >> password;
        ofstream saveFile;
```

```cpp
    saveFile.open("D:\\reg.txt", ios::app
| ios::binary);
    if (!saveFile)
    {
        cout << "File can't be opened\n";
    }
    else
    {
        cout<<"\n";
        saveFile.write((char *)&obj[id],
sizeof(EmailData));
        saveFile.close();
    }
    cout << "Registration completed";
}

int main()
{
    cout << "User 1 :: \n";
    obj[0].reg(0);
    cout << "User 2 :: \n";
    obj[1].reg(1);
    cout << "User 3 :: \n";
    obj[2].reg(2);

    EmailData emailData;

    ifstream saveFile;
    saveFile.open("D:\\reg.txt", ios::in |
ios::binary);
    if (!saveFile)
    {
        cout << "Cannot read file\n";
    }
    else
    {
```

```
            cout << "Users:\n";
            saveFile.read((char *)&emailData,
sizeof(emailData));
            while (saveFile)
            {
                cout << "Username:" <<
emailData.username << "\nPasswword:" <<
emailData.password << "\n";
                saveFile.read((char
*)&emailData, sizeof(emailData));
            }
            //saveFile.close();
        }
        return 0;
}
```

As a result, the previous coding will look like this:

```
Enter Registration Details for User 1 ::

Enter user name :: Username1

Enter password :: Nameofwebsite.com


..........You are now registered.........


Enter Registration Details for User 2 ::

Enter user name :: John

Enter password :: Mackey


..........You are now registered.........
```

```
Enter Registration Details for User 3 ::

Enter user name :: Miles

Enter password :: Pacino


..........You are now registered.........


Registered Details of All Users ::

Username:: Username1
Passwword:: Nameofwebsite.com

Username:: John
Passwword:: Mackey

Username:: Miles
Passwword:: Pacino
```

14.3 Banking System Project

The account class in this banking system C ++ software provides data members including such account no, deposit account, name withdrawal amount, and account type. The customer's information is recorded inside a binary file. A consumer's account can be used to deposit and make withdrawals. Accounts may be created, modified, and deleted by the user. Here are some easy examples to help you start building a banking system.

To create an account, you can start with this module:

```
void write_account()
```

```
{
    CustomerAccount customerAccount;
    ofstream customerAccountFile;
    CustomerAccount.open ("CustomerAccount.
dat", ios::binary | ios::app);
    customerAccount.create_account ();
    CustomerAccount.write (reinterpret_cast
<char *> (&customerAccount),
sizeof (CustomerAccount));
    CustomerAccount.close ();
}
```

With and Deposit:

void AcountWithdrawAndDeposit(int n, int choice)

```
{
    int amount;
    bool customerFound = false;
    CustomerAccount customerAccount;
    fstream CustomerData;
    CustomerData.open ("CustomerAccount.dat
", ios::binary | ios::in | ios::out);
    if (!CustomerData)
    {
        cout << "Cant Open File";
        return;
    }
    while (!CustomerData.eof () &&
customerFound == false)
    {

    CustomerData.read (reinterpret_cast<cha
r *> (&customerAccount),
sizeof (CustomerAccount));
    if (customerAccount.retacno () == n)
```

```cpp
        {
customerAccount.show_account();
            if (choice == 1)
            {
        cout << "Deposit Amount\n ";
            cout << "Enter amount";
                cin >> amount;
        customerAccount.dep(amount);
            }
            if (choice == 2)
            {
            cout << "Withdraw Amount ";
            cout << "Enter amount";
                cin >> amount;
        int bal = customerAccount.retdeposit()
- amount;
        if ((bal < 500 &&
customerAccount.rettype() == 'S') || (bal <
1000 && customerAccount.rettype() == 'C'))
        cout << "Not enough amount in
account";
                    else
            customerAccount.draw(amount);
                }
        int pos = (-
1)*static_cast<int>(sizeof(customerAccount))
;
        CustomerData.seekp(pos, ios::cur);
        CustomerData.write(reinterpret_cast<ch
ar *> (&customerAccount),
sizeof(CustomerAccount));
                cout << "Data Updated";
                customerFound = true;
            }
        }
        CustomerData.close();
```

```
        if (customerFound == false)
            cout << "Customer Not Found in
data file";
}
```

Show Balance :

```
void display_sp(int n)
{
    CustomerAccount customerAccount;
    bool cutomerFound = false;
    ifstream CustomerData;
    CustomerData.open("CustomerAccount.dat
", ios::binary);
    if (!CustomerData)
    {
        cout << "File Cannot be opened.";
        return;
    }
    cout << "Account details\n";
    while
(CustomerData.read(reinterpret_cast<char *>
(&customerAccount),
sizeof(CustomerAccount)))
    {
    if (customerAccount.retacno() == n)
        {
        customerAccount.show_account();
            cutomerFound = true;
        }
    }
    CustomerData.close();
    if (cutomerFound == false)
        cout << "Account in not present
in data file";
}
```

14.4 Guess the Casino's Numbers

This is an exciting project that will teach us regarding the cstdlib package., which is used to generate random numbers. The application first asks the user for a betting sum, after which it asks him or her to estimate a number that will be rolled. If the randomly generated number matches the user's input, the user wins; otherwise, money is removed from his account. The user has the option to continue playing until he has lost all of the money he originally invested.

The code structure below demonstrates:

```cpp
#include <iostream>
#include <string>
#include <cstdlib>
#include <ctime>
using namespace std;

void paintLine(int count, char s)
{
        for (int i = 0; i < count; i++)
            cout << s;
        cout << "\n";
}

void GameRules()
{
        system("cls");
        paintLine(60, '-');
        cout << "Rules\n";
        paintLine(60, '-');
        cout << "1. Pick number from 1 to
10\n";
```

```cpp
        cout << "2. On correct gameChoice you
will have 10 time of money\n";
        cout << "3. On wrong gameChoice you
will lose betting money\n";
        paintLine(60, '-');
}

int main()
{
        string gamePlayer;
        int gameAmount;
        int gameBettingAmount;
        int gameGuess;
        int gameDice;
        char gameChoice;

        srand(time(0));

        paintLine(50, '_');
        cout << "\tGAME\n";
        paintLine(50, '_');

        cout << "Name of gamePlayer: ";
        getline(cin, gamePlayer);

        cout << "\n\nEnter Deposit gameAmount
to play game : $";
        cin >> gameAmount;

        do
        {
                system("cls");
                GameRules();
                cout << "Total balance is Rs " <<
gameAmount << "\n";
                do
```

137

```cpp
        {
                cout << gamePlayer << ",
Write amount for bet : Rs";
                cin >> gameBettingAmount;
                if (gameBettingAmount >
gameAmount)
                        cout << "Amount for
bet is more than total balance\n"
                        << "\nEnter again the
betting amount\n ";
        } while (gameBettingAmount >
gameAmount);

        do
        {
                cout << "Guess your number
to bet between 1 to 10 :";
                cin >> gameGuess;
                if (gameGuess <= 0 ||
gameGuess > 10)
                        cout << "Please check
the number!! should be between 1 to 10\n"
                        << "\nRe-enter data\n ";
        } while (gameGuess <= 0 ||
gameGuess > 10);

        gameDice = rand() % 10 + 1;

        if (gameDice == gameGuess)
        {
                cout << "You won Rs." <<
gameBettingAmount * 10;
                gameAmount = gameAmount +
gameBettingAmount * 10;
        }
        else
```

```cpp
        {
            cout << "You lost Rs " <<
gameBettingAmount << "\n";
                gameAmount = gameAmount -
gameBettingAmount;
        }

        cout << "\nOriginal number was :
" << gameDice << "\n";
            cout << "\n" << gamePlayer << ",
Remaining Amount Rs " << gameAmount << "\n";
            if (gameAmount == 0)
            {
                cout << "You have no money
to play ";
                break;
            }
            cout << "play again (y/n)? ";
            cin >> gameChoice;
        } while (gameChoice == 'Y' ||
gameChoice == 'y');
        cout << "\n\n\n";
        paintLine(70, '=');
        cout << "Your balance gameAmount is Rs
" << gameAmount << "\n";
        paintLine(70, '=');

        return 0;
}
```

14.5 Employee Record System

Employee Record System (ERS) is a computerized system that
enables businesses to manage their staff members along with their
records. It can be utilized by any size business, whether it has 10 or
1000 members in its staff.

Here is the C program for the Employee recording system:

```c
#pragma warning(disable : 4996)
#include <stdio.h>
#include <stdlib.h>
#include <string.h>
#include <windows.h>
#include <conio.h>

struct emp {
    char empName[50];
    float empSalary;
    int empAge;
    int empId;
};
struct emp emp;

long int empSize = sizeof(emp);

FILE *fp, *ft;


void deleteentry()
{
    system("cls");
    char empName[50];
    char again = 'y';

    while (again == 'y') {
        printf("\nEnter employee name: ");
        scanf("%s", empName);

        ft = fopen("temp.txt", "wb");
        rewind(fp);
```

```c
            while (fread(&emp, empSize,
                1, fp)
                == 1) {
                if (strcmp(emp.empName,
                    empName)
                    != 0)
            fwrite(&emp, empSize, 1, ft);
            }
            fclose(fp);
            fclose(ft);
            remove("EmployeeDataFile.txt");
        rename("temp.txt",
"EmployeeDataFile.txt");
            fp =
fopen("EmployeeDataFile.txt", "rb+");
        printf("delete another ?(Y/N) :");
            fflush(stdin);
            again = getch();
        }
}
void displayentry()
{
        system("cls");
        rewind(fp);

        printf("\nEmployee Name\t\tEmployee
Age\t\tEmployee Salary\t\t"
            "\tEmployee ID\n",
            emp.empName, emp.empAge,
            emp.empSalary, emp.empId);
while (fread(&emp, empSize, 1, fp) == 1)
        printf("\n%s\t\t%d\t\t%.2f\t%10d",
                emp.empName, emp.empAge,
emp.empSalary, emp.empId);
        printf("\n");
        system("pause");
```

```
}
void modifyentry()
{
    system("cls");
    char empName[50];
    char again = 'y';
    while (again == 'y') {
        printf("Employee name : ");
        scanf("%s", empName);
        rewind(fp);
        while (fread(&emp, empSize, 1,
fp) == 1) {
            if (strcmp(emp.empName,
empName) == 0) {
                printf("New name:");
                scanf("%s", emp.empName);
                printf("New age :");
                scanf("%d", &emp.empAge);
                printf("New Salary :");
                scanf("%f", &emp.empSalary);
                printf("New ID :");
                scanf("%d", &emp.empId);
                fseek(fp, -empSize, SEEK_CUR);
                fwrite(&emp, empSize, 1, fp);
                break;
            }
        }
        printf("modify another record
(Y/N) :");
        fflush(stdin);
        scanf("%c", &again);
    }
}
void addentry()
{
    system("cls");
```

```c
        fseek(fp, 0, SEEK_END);
        char again = 'y';
        while (again == 'y') {
        printf("\nEnter Employee Name : ");
               scanf("%s", emp.empName);
        printf("\nEnter Employee Age : ");
               scanf("%d", &emp.empAge);
        printf("\nEnter Employee Salary : ");
               scanf("%f", &emp.empSalary);
               printf("\nEnter Employee Id : ");
               scanf("%d", &emp.empId);
               fwrite(&emp, empSize, 1, fp);
               printf("add another employee?"
                    " record (Y/N) : ");
               fflush(stdin);
               scanf("%c", &again);
        }
}
int main()
{
        int option;
fp = fopen("EmployeeDataFile.txt", "rb+");
        if (fp == NULL) {
fp = fopen("EmployeeDataFile.txt", "wb+");
            if (fp == NULL) {
        printf("\nCan't open file...");
               exit(1);
               }
        }
        printf("EMPLOYEE Database\n");
        system("pause");
        while (1) {
               system("cls");
               printf("1. New Entry\n");
               printf("2. Delete Entry\n");
               printf("3. Display Entry\n");
```

```c
            printf("4. Modify Entry\n");
            printf("5. Close Program\n");
            printf("Enter option...\n");
            fflush(stdin);
            scanf("%d", &option);
            switch (option) {
            case 1:
                  addentry();
                  break;
            case 2:
                  deleteentry();
                  break;
            case 3:
                  displayentry();
                  break;
            case 4:
                  modifyentry();
                  break;
            case 5:
                  fclose(fp);
                  exit(0);
                  break;
            default:
                  printf("Wrong option.\n");
            }
      }
      return 0;
}
```

Conclusion

Thank you so much for purchasing this book. C ++ is a language that is widely used, particularly in-system programs and embedded devices. System programming refers to the creation of operating systems and drivers that interact with hardware. Automobiles, robots, and appliances are examples of embedded systems. It has a larger or richer developer community, which facilitates the employment of development companies and online solutions.

Because of its security and features, C ++ is touted to it as the smartest language. It's the first language that each developer should learn if they want to work with this language. And is very simple for learning since it is a basic principle language. The fairly basic syntax is, making it simple to write and develop, and faults are quickly repeated. Before learning some other languages, programmers wanted to study (C ++) first, followed by additional languages. However, most developers choose C ++ because of its versatility and interoperability with a broad range of systems and software.

Good Luck!